Andrea Pomella

VATICAN MUSEUMS

EDIZIONI MUSEI VATICANI

PRESENTATION

It is most certainly a happy coincidence that this excellent publication by Andrea Pomella should appear in the same year the Vatican Museums are celebrating their 500th anniversary.

Although a merely conventional date - it is, in fact, the fifth centenary of the discovery of the marble group of Laocoon, the first of the many sculptures which, in the first half of the 16th century, gave life to the Courtyard of the Statues and, in a broader sense, to the art collections of the Roman Pontiffs - this anniversary serves to remind us of the historic importance and the spiritual and cultural function of this collection, which has been on public display for over two centuries.

The complex history of the Vatican Museums, so well summarised in this volume, closely reflects the changing contexts and the political, cultural and social developments that have succeeded one another down the centuries. What emerges is the profile of an Institution in many ways unique on the international cultural scene, open like few others to the rest of the world but, at the same time, aware and proud of its specific nature as the Museums of the Popes.

The publication of practical, accurate, well-documented and illustrated works is an important way to give our visitors a more complete and up-to-date understanding of the masterpieces kept in the Vatican Museums and Palaces.

We are well aware that in a world in constant demand of culture, communication is just as important for popular as for academic purposes. It is essential, however, to maintain high-quality publications, while respecting both the printed works and the reading public. Andrea Pomella's book responds well to these needs as he also describes, alongside the traditional sights to be seen during a tour of the Museums, the new architectural areas opened for the Jubilee Year 2000 and the new works commissioned at that time.

Francesco Buranelli
Director of the Vatican Museums

The foundations of the Vatican Museums lie in the patronage of the arts of the humanist popes of the second half of the 15ᵗʰ century, and in the collections they assembled. During that time, art, as part of the Church's theological and political designs, became the most sublime form for propagating and preserving the faith; an ideal translated into the pontifical rooms and chapels through the works of the main artists of that time.

The dominant cultural trend of the early Renaissance was a continuous aspiration towards the insuperable perfection of the ancients in every form of art. In this context, Greco-Roman classical culture attained its most consummate expression as the language of art conformed to the themes of Christian experience.

The nucleus of the new enthusiasm for collecting art was the courtyard of the *Palazzetto del Belvedere* of Pope Innocent VIII (1484-1492). Here Cardinal Giuliano della Rovere, the most far-sighted of patrons of arts and culture who later became Pope Julius II (1503-1513), placed a real "miracle of art": the *Apollo*, known as "Belvedere", discovered near Grottaferrata in 1489. The courtyard was altered in the 16ᵗʰ century to accommodate a garden, and was decorated with further important classical statues. Among these were the *Laocoon*, discovered in the *Domus Aurea*; the *Venus Felix*, a statue of a Roman woman depicted as Venus probably found in the basilica of Santa Croce in Gerusalemme; the *Nile* and the *Tiber*, colossal marbles found in the Temple of Isis (*Iseo Campese*); and the statue of *Hercules with the*

young Thelephus found in Campo de' Fiori.

During the 17ᵗʰ century, with the Counter-Reformation and its cultural and moral implications, the growth of the Vatican collections came to a standstill. Their development and arrangement continued only in the 18ᵗʰ century, when intellectuals began to take more interest in the gracefulness of art, aesthetic philosophy and the cult of the preservation of beauty. To Popes Clement XIV (1769-1774) and Pius VI (1775-1799) goes the honour of having arranged a collection of classical antiquities in the Vatican, which served not only as a testimony to the ancient world but also, and above all, stood out for the rational manner in which the works were arranged and exhibited. Known as the *Pio-Clementino*, this museum also served to safeguard a priceless artistic heritage from the constant threat of being exported en masse. To this nucleus Pius VII (1800-1823) later added the *Chiaramonti Museum* and the *Braccio Nuovo*.

During the 19ᵗʰ century, under the influence of the Romantic Movement, attention shifted to civilisations which until then had been considered as foreign and distant from the classical world. Intense excavation work, especially in southern Etruria, brought these civilisations to light in all

Chiaramonti Museum,
Francesco Hayez, Allegory for the return to Rome of the works of art from the Papal States
left, *Museums of the Vatican Apostolic Library,*
Clementine Gallery, Anonymous, Pius VII in 1815 purchases a series of Etruscan vases to enrich the Museums of the Library

their magnificence. The *Etruscan Museum* dates back to 1836 and the *Egyptian Museum* to 1839, both were favoured during the pontificate of Gregory XVI (1831-1846).

In the 20th century, the classical age was celebrated in the *Lateran Museum of Pagan Antiquities*, today called the *Gregorian Profane Museum*. It was created in 1844 to exhibit Roman finds. Pius IX (1846-1878) later added the *Pio-Christian Museum* which exhibited late-ancient and early Christian art. In 1960, John XXIII (1958-1963) ordered that both museums be moved from the Lateran Palace to the Vatican where they were placed in a specially-constructed building which also houses the *Ethnological Missionary Museum*, created in 1926. The *Modern Religious Art Collection* is more recent. It was established by Paul VI during his pontificate (1963-1978) with the aim of re-awakening dialogue between the Catholic Church and contemporary artists.

The Vatican Museums also house the *Vatican Pinacoteca*, the *Upper Galleries* (including the *Gallery of the Candelabra*, the *Gallery of Tapestries* and the *Gallery of Maps*), the *Museums of the Vatican Apostolic Library*, the *Sobieski Room* and the *Sala dell'Immacolata*.

To these must be added other features of notable artistic and cultur-

al excellence, found in the Vatican Palaces, such as the *Sistine Chapel*, the *Stanze* and *Loggias of Raphael*, and the *Chapel of Nicholas V* frescoed by Fra Angelico.

In the Jubilee 2000, the Vatican Museums were equipped with a modern and monumental entrance, "one of the most significant doors of the Holy See open to the world" as John Paul II (1978-2005) defined it in his inaugural address. The entrance leads to a remarkable spiral ramp, set on an inclined plane, which links the entrance to the exhibition areas on the upper floors. The atrium contains various artworks, among them a large 1st-century polychrome mosaic from a Roman villa on the Via Ardeatina, and two works by contemporary artists: the new bronze door itself, by the sculptor Cecco Bonanotte, and a white marble sculpture by Giuliano Vangi called *Crossing the Threshold*.

This book offers readers an overview of the Vatican Museums, in the light of the transformations they have undergone over the centuries, along with the purchases made, and the historical and artistic events which brought them to their present arrangement. Furthermore, it aims to underline the importance of the immense artistic and religious heritage preserved in each of the exhibition areas.

Spiral ramp leading to the Vatican Museums,
inaugurated in the Jubilee 2000
left, *New entrance to the Vatican Museums*

PINACOTECA

The Vatican Pinacoteca derives from a picture gallery set up under the pontificate of Pius VI (1775-1799) in what is now the Gallery of Tapestries. Initially the collection comprised about a hundred paintings dating from the 16th century onwards. It was later enlarged with many other acquisitions, legacies and donations. Some sections, such as the "primitives" and the Greek and Slavic icons, were taken from the Vatican Apostolic Library and the altars inside St Peter's Basilica. Others came from the Gallery of the Lateran Pontifical Palace, founded in 1844. Many of these masterpieces were removed to Paris following the Treaty of Tolentino in 1797. Some paintings were brought back to Italy following Napoleon's defeat at Waterloo and the subsequent decisions of the Congress of Vienna in 1815, which ordered the restitution of those works of art taken by the French from the defeated countries. Pius VII (1800-1823) had these works placed in the rooms of the Borgia Apartment.

The collection had five nuclei: paintings from Pius VI's Gallery (recovered in Paris and from the Quirinal Palace, a papal residence until 1870), works taken from churches of Rome and the Pontifical States, paintings moved from the Capitoline Gallery on the Capitol (founded in the mid 18th

century and housing the Sacchetti and Pio di Savoia collections), and classical art paintings and works of various origins.

Having been moved several times within the Museums and Apostolic Palaces, the collection finally came to rest in the Vatican Pinacoteca, inaugurated in a structure purpose-built by Pius XI (1922-1939) in 1932. The building, with its eclectic style inspired by Renaissance architecture, was the work of architect Luca Beltrami. It conformed to the modern museological concepts of that period.

Today the Vatican Pinacoteca houses more than 400 paintings in eighteen rooms, the last three added after 1984. Many paintings have religious subjects, though there is no lack of important non-religious ones, such as the *Portrait of George IV of England* by Thomas Lawrence and the magnificent works of the Austrian animalist Wenzel Peter, who also painted *Adam and Eve in the Garden of Eden* in Room XVI. Other foreign painters include Lucas Cranach the Elder, Poussin, and Van Dyck, while Italian paintings are represented by major artists including Giotto, Filippo Lippi, Melozzo da Forlì, Perugino, Raphael, Leonardo, Caravaggio and Titian. The paintings are exhibited in chronological order and by school, from the Middle Ages to 1800. In the past, the Pinacoteca also had works by contemporary painters, but these have now been moved to the Collection of Modern Religious Art, which was specially created by Paul VI (1963-1978) in 1973 and contains a vast number of paintings, sculptures and works of graphic art.

Pinacoteca,
Room II, Lorenzo Monaco, St Anthony Abbot meets Paul the Hermit
left, Room XII, Guido Reni, St Matthew and Angel
pages 10 and 11, Room XVI, Wenzel Peter, Adam and Eve in the Garden of Eden

+ REGNVM PERCIPITE BENEDICTI QVIQ VENITE · VOBIS PARATVM PER SECLA CVNCTA DONATVM ·

+ OFFERET VT PAVLVS FVERIT Q DO VIS Q LVCRATVS · QD MARTYR STEPHANVS CLAMAT GREX ISTE PVSILLV · MEQ APAVISTI POTV PSEPE DEDISTI · VEL SI MVI IN DVTO REPARASTI CORPORE NVDS ·

C ME GENVS VOLVCRV VEL REPTILIS ATQ FERARV · REDDVNT HVMANA PISCES QVOQ MENBRA VORATA ·

TIS EST · · · ES PARADISIO · · · · HOS · · · · · · · · · · · · · · · · · BLISIRA

GREXISTEPVSILLV MEQAPA VISTIPOTVPSEPEDEDISTIVE
NEREREGNEDANSQVOOSTARTAREINIVSTOSINFIMACLAVSTEHO

HVMANA PISCESQVOQ MENBRA VORATA

Room I contains works by Italian mediaeval artists, the so-called "primitives". Among the works, mostly in tempera on wood, is the remarkable *Last Judgement* by Nicolò and Giovanni (Roman school of the second half of the 12th century), a round painting with a rectangular base from the oratory of St Gregory Nazianzeno near St Mary's in Campo Marzio in Rome. The iconography is divided into tiers positioned one on top of the other, separated by subtitles. Starting from the top, Christ Pantocrator enthroned between angels and seraphs; below, Christ in priestly robes prays before an altar between the Apostles and with the tools of the Passion. The third register has three scenes: on the left, Dysmas "the good thief" with the cross in his hand ahead of St Paul who guides those risen from the dead, then the Virgin and St Stephen interceding for the Holy Innocents and, finally, three of the seven Works of Mercy (clothe the naked, visit the imprisoned, give drink to the thirsty). Below this is the Resurrec-

tion of the Dead: on the left stand those devoured by wild animals and fish, on the right, the calling of the dead from their tombs, and in the centre, the allegories of Earth and Sea. At the bottom are depictions of Hell and the damned (right), and the Celestial Jerusalem (Paradise) with the Virgin flanked by two Saints and surrounded by the elect (left). Below the Virgin are portraits of the two nuns who commissioned the painting, identified by the title as "Domna Benedicta ancilla Dei" and "Costantia abbatissa". Apart from this work and the *Stefaneschi Triptych* (Room II), all the paintings in the first two Rooms of the Pinacoteca come from the Vatican Apostolic Library.

Room II houses temperas from the age of Giotto and the late Gothic

Pinacoteca, Room I, Nicolò and Giovanni,
The Last Judgement, detail
left, *The Last Judgement*

period, including one of the most important masterpieces in the Vatican Pinacoteca, the *Stefaneschi Triptych*, a work by Giotto and his pupils from the basilica of St Peter. Commissioned by Cardinal Jacopo Stefaneschi around 1320 for the main altar, it is made up of three sections and a predella, painted on both sides. *Recto*: in the centre, St Peter enthroned among angels and offerers (Cardinal Stefaneschi is shown being introduced by St George, while Pope Celestine V, in a monk's habit, by St Sylvester, both intent on offering Peter a small model of the triptych and a manuscript); on the side panels, St James and St Paul on the left, St Andrew and St John the Evangelist on the right. The only surviving panel of the predella shows St Stephen and two Saints. *Verso*: in the centre, Christ enthroned with Angels and a supplicant at his feet (Stefaneschi himself); to the sides, the Crucifixion of St Peter and the Beheading of St Paul. The three sections of the predella show, in the centre, the Virgin and Child enthroned between Angels, St Peter and St James and, on each side, five Apostles. Other works in this room include the *Redeemer conferring a Blessing*, a small painting (probably a cymatium of a polyptych) attributed to Simone Martini, a Sienese artist of the first half of the 14th century, considered one of the major innovators of late mediaeval art.

The section of 15th-century paintings comprises works from the Vatican Apostolic Library, the collection of the Holy Congregation *De Propaganda Fide* (mostly from the Ferrieri donation) and the Lateran collection. All are tempera or oil paintings by painters from Siena, Florence, Umbria-Marches, Ferrara, the Venice region and from central Italy, with the exception of two examples from the Rhine School (the *Martyrdom of St Bartholomew* and the *Martyrdom of Sts Simon and Jude*) and the famous *Pietà* by Lucas Cranach the Elder.

Room III houses mostly works by Filippo Lippi, Fra Angelico and Benozzo Gazzoli. The great triptych of the *Crowning of the Virgin, angels, saints and donors*, completed around 1460 for the chapel of St Bernard in the convent of the *Olivetane* nuns at Arezzo is by Filippo Lippi and his assistants. The painting shows Gregorio Marsuppini and his son Carlo (who commissioned the work) as donors, introduced to the contemplation of the event by St Gregory and saintly monks. Fra Angelico is thought to be the painter of the *Stories of St Nicholas of Bari*, sections from the predella of a large triptych made about 1437 for the chapel of St Nicholas in the church of St Dominic in Perugia, and today held at the National Gallery of Umbria in Perugia. Of the two panels in the Vatican, one represents the birth and vocation of the Saint and his gift to the three poor girls; the other shows St Nicholas meeting an imperial legate, the rescue of a corn cargo for the town of Myra and the mir-

Pinacoteca, Room II, Giotto and assistants, Stefaneschi Triptych (verso)

243   FRA FILIPPO LIPPI 1406-1469
           L'INCORONAZIONE DELLA VERGINE

Pinacoteca, Room III, Filippo Lippi and assistants,
Crowning of the Virgin, angels, saints and donors
above, *Crowning of the Virgin, angels, saints and donors, detail*
pages 20 and 21, *Room III, Fra Angelico, Stories of St Nicholas of Bari:*
Birth of the Saint, Vocation, Gift to the three poor girls

TEMPLA DOMVM EXPOSITIS:VICOS:FORA:MOENIA:PONTES:
VIRGINEAM TRIVII QVOD REPARARIS AQVAM.
PRISCA LICET NAVTIS STATVAS DARE COMMODA PORTVS:
ET VATICANVM CINGERE SIXTE IVGVM:
PLVS TAMEN VRBS DEBET:NAM QVAE SQVALORE LATEBAT:
CERNITVR IN CELEBRI BIBLIOTHECA LOCO.

acle of a ship saved from sinking. The *Virgin presenting the girdle to St Thomas*, known as the "Madonna of the Girdle", a work by Gozzoli, was painted in 1452 for the main altar of the collegiate church of St Fortunatus in Montefalco. The altarpiece shows the Virgin above the clouds surrounded by angels and cherubs with the saint at her feet; on the predella are six episodes from Mary's life, beginning from the left: birth, Annunciation, marriage, birth of Christ, disputation in the Temple, her death.

Room IV contains works by Melozzo da Forlì and his assistant Marco Palmezzano. Melozzo produced the great fresco dedicated to *Sixtus IV and Platina*, transferred onto canvas from the rooms of the Vatican Apostolic Library, which Sixtus IV had founded in 1475. It was the central episode of a cycle of paintings, also entrusted to Antoniazzo and the brothers Domenico and Davide Ghirlandaio, for the decoration of the Library. It shows an enthroned Sixtus IV in the act of appointing the kneeling Bartolomeo Sacchi, known as "Platina", as first Prefect of the Vatican Apostolic Library. Beside the Vicar of Christ are his cardinal nephews Pietro Riario (whom many see as the proto-notary Raffaele) and Giuliano della Rovere (the future Pope Julius II) in his cardinal robes, and his lay nephews Giovanni della Rovere and Girolamo Riario. Also by this artist are the fragments with *angels musicians* and *heads of Apostles*, which were taken, together with the *Redeemer conferring a Blessing* exhibited in the Quirinal Palace, from the apsidal fresco of ca. 1480 in the Roman basilica of the Holy Apostles. Among Palmezzano's paintings is

Pinacoteca, Room IV, Melozzo da Forlì, Sixtus IV and Platina, detail
left, *Sixtus IV and Platina*

the altarpiece dedicated to the *Madonna and Child with Sts Francis, Lawrence, John the Baptist, Peter, Dominic and Anthony Abbot*. It is a late oil panting on wood completed by the artist in 1537 for the church of the convent of the Carmine in Cesena.

Room V houses works by 15th-century Italian and foreign artists. Apart from one in glazed terracotta, all are tempera or oil works on canvas and wood. They include the *Miracles of St Vincent Ferrer* by Ercole de' Roberti and the later *Pietà* by Lucas Cranach the Elder, from the Kreuzlingen Convent of the Canons Regular of St Augustine. The work by de' Roberti is the predella to an altarpiece by his master, Francesco del Cossa, for the Griffoni Chapel in St Petronius in Bologna around 1473. It was dismantled at the end of the 18th century. The miracles are narrated in linear sequence, linked uninterruptedly in time and space: St Vincent heals a lame woman, raises a rich Spanish Jewish woman from the dead, saves a child from a burning house, raises a dead child killed by his insane mother, heals a man with an injured leg.

Room VI is dedicated to polyptychs of the second half of the 15th century. There are many paintings on display, including the *Crucifixion with Sts Venantius, Peter, John the Baptist and Porphyry* (known as the "Camerino Triptych" as it came from the collegiate church of St Venantius in Camerino), and the *Crowning of the Virgin, Christ deposed and*

Pinacoteca, Room V, Ercole de' Roberti,
Miracles of St Vincent Ferrer
right, *Miracles of St Vincent Ferrer, detail*

saints or the "Montelparo Polyptych", transferred from the church of St Michael the Archangel in Castello di Montelparo. Both works are by Niccolò di Liberatore, known as "the Pupil", and have ornate Gothic frames testifying to the influence of Venetian culture. There is also a *Pietà* by Carlo Crivelli, a lunette cymatium from the Italian Marches, although its exact origin is unknown; and the *Crowning of the Virgin, Nativity, Adoration of the Magi* (known as the "Rospigliosi Triptych"), painted by Bartolomeo di Tommaso around 1450, and given by Prince Altieri to Leo XIII for his priestly ordination jubilee (1888).

Room VII houses works of the Umbrian school, including paintings by such important artists as Pinturicchio and Perugino, who worked especially with tempera on canvas or wood. The *Crowning of the Virgin,* a tempera on wood that was later transferred to canvas, is an altarpiece dating from 1503, painted by Pinturicchio in collaboration with Giovan Battista Caporali for the convent of St Mary of the Friars Minor Observant (Franciscans) at Umbertide; Perugino's is the *Madonna and Child with Sts Herculanus, Constance, Lawrence and Ludwig of Toulouse* (the "Decemviri Altarpiece"), an altarpiece from 1496 commissioned by the Decemviri of Perugia for the chapel of the Priori Palace. It originally formed a cymatium showing *Christ in Pietà*, now in the National Gallery of Umbria.

The following Rooms of the Pinacoteca are dedicated to the 16th-century collection. It comprises works of the Venetian school, a small number from Lombardy, paintings by Barocci, and examples from other schools including the Roman. Most of these works come from Pius VII's picture gallery and include Raphael Sanzio's paintings which were returned from Paris.

Room VIII is entirely dedicated to works by Raphael. The walls are hung with tapestries – woven to drawings by the artist and his school – while the central space is dominated by three altarpieces in tempera on wood, also by the master from Urbino. They are the *Crowning of the Virgin* (or "Oddi Altarpiece") dated ca. 1513 from the chapel of the Oddi family in the church of San Francesco al Prato in Perugia; the *Madonna of Foligno* from ca. 1511, so called after it was transferred from the church of Aracoeli in Rome to the church of the Monastery of St Ann of the Countesses of Foligno (these first two works have been transferred onto canvas); and finally, the *Transfiguration* of 1520. The first of these works shows Christ crowning the Virgin, who is surrounded by angel musicians, while the Apostles, standing around the flowered tomb, watch the event from below. The predella depicts the Annunciation, the Adoration of the Magi and the Presentation of Jesus in the Temple.

Pinacoteca, Room V, Lucas Cranach the Elder, Pietà
pages 28 and 29, *Room VI, Carlo Crivelli, Pietà*

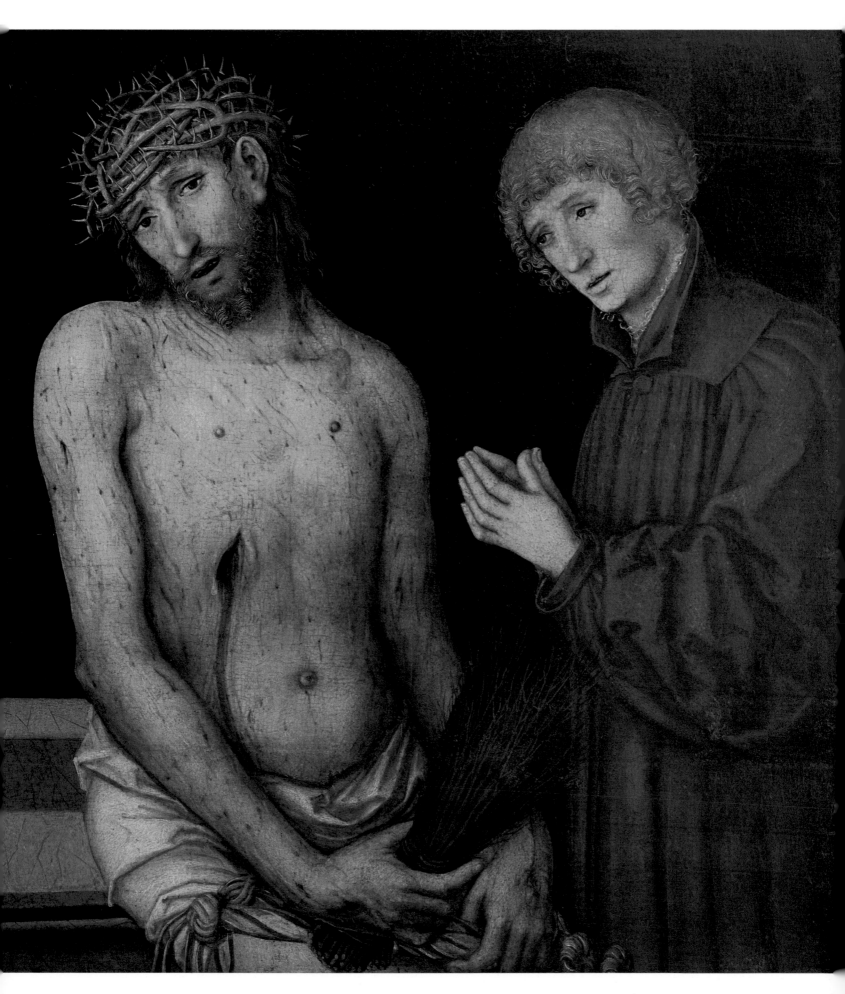

OPVS·CAROLI·CRIVELLI·VENETI·

In the second work St Jerome introduces to the Madonna, seated in glory, the kneeling Sigismondo de' Conti (who commissioned the work), grateful to her for having saved his house from lightning (an episode visible in the background of the painting). The third work belongs to Raphael's late period: in the upper part is Christ transfigured between Moses and Elijah, and Peter, John and James; in the lower part, the episode of the possessed boy meeting the Apostles. The underlying theme is that grace can only be achieved through Faith, here represented by the kneeling woman in the foreground.

Room IX is a small room housing works by Leonardo da Vinci and various 16th-century artists. Giovanni Bellini painted the *Lament over the dead Christ with Sts Joseph of Arimathaea, Nicodemus and Mary*

Magdalene, the cymatium of an altarpiece from ca. 1474 for the main altar of the church of St Francis in Pesaro. Today, the altarpiece is kept in the Civic Museum. The solemn composition shows Christ surrounded by Mary Magdalene, Nicodemus and Joseph of Arimathaea.

The most famous painting is however the monochrome *St Jerome* by Leonardo, a late 15th-century oil on wood ascribed to the artist's early

Pinacoteca, Room VII,
Perugino, Madonna and Child with Sts Ercolanus, Constance,
Lawrence and Ludwig of Toulouse, detail
left, *Pinturicchio and Giovan Battista Caporali, Crowning of the Virgin*

Pinacoteca, Room VIII, Raphael,
Crowning of the Virgin
left and above,
Crowning of the Virgin, details

Pinacoteca, Room VIII, Raphael, Madonna of Foligno
left and above, *Madonna of Foligno, details*

Pinacoteca, Room VIII, Raphael, Transfiguration
left and above, *Transfiguration, details*

37

Florentine period. The saint is kneeling, his head inclined, his gaunt and imploring frame captures the embodiment of ascesis and mortification. At his feet is a ravenous lion of which only the outline remains, while the facade of the Florentine church of Santa Maria Novella can be seen in the background. The painting was broken up and lost following the artist's death. It was recomposed only in the late 18th century when the pieces were found by chance being used as a box lid in a second-hand dealer's shop and as a cover for a cobbler's stool.

Room X contains works by Titian and 16th-century Venetian paintings, beautifully executed oils on canvas and wood. Titian painted the *Portrait of Doge Niccolò Marcello*, from around 1542, once part of the Aldrovandi collection of Bologna, and the *Madonna with Child and Saints*, from around 1535, better known as "Madonna of the Frari" as it came from the oratory of the church of San Niccolò della Lattuga in Campo dei Frari in Venice. The altarpiece, originally on wood and later transferred to canvas, is divided into two parts: in the upper, the Virgin with Child and angels; in the lower, Sts Catherine of Alexandria, Nicholas, Peter, Anthony of Padua, Francis and Sebastian. There are two works by Veronese from the Pio di Savoia collection: the *Allegory of the Liberal Arts*, an octagonal painting (probably a ceiling decoration) from about 1551, and the *Vision of St Helen* from around 1580, a painting dedicated to the dream-vision of the saint who legend says found the True Cross. Paris Bordon painted *St George killing the Dragon*, a work commissioned for the high altar of the parish church of St Francis of Noale around 1525.

Room XI is dedicated to late 16th-century artists. Ludovico Carracci painted the *Trinity with the dead Christ and angels showing the tools of the Passion* of ca. 1590, which was in Cardinal Flavio Chigi's collection and was probably a cymatium over an altarpiece or above a sacristy door. Giorgio Vasari's is the *Stoning of St Stephen*, a huge altarpiece painted in 1571 for the chapel of St Stephen which is located in a wing of the Pontifical Palace built by Pius V (1566-1572). Federico Barrocci painted the *Rest during the Flight into Egypt* (known as the "Madonna of the Cherries"), a beautifully chromatic painting commissioned from the artist by Simonetto Anastagi of Perugia around 1573, and the *Annunciation*, an altarpiece completed around 1584 for the chapel of Francesco Maria II della Rovere, Duke of Urbino, in the basilica of Loreto. This canvas however has been much repainted due both to damage suffered during transportation and to poor restorations. In the background of the scene is a night view of Valbona (a district of Urbino) and the western side of the Ducal Palace.

Pinacoteca, Room IX, Giovanni Bellini,
Lament over the dead Christ with Sts Joseph of Arimathaea,
Nicodemus and Mary Magdalene

The area dedicated to 17th century paintings contains important works by the most representative artists from many places, especially those active in the artistic life of Rome: oils on canvas and wood brought to the Vatican Pinacoteca from the basilica of St Peter and the churches of Rome, the Vatican Apartments, the Pontifical Palace of Castelgandolfo and through various acquisitions. Alongside this nucleus is a small collection of lay and religious paintings dating from the 18th century.

Room XII is an octagonal space housing important oil paintings by early Baroque artists. Among the works is the *Crucifixion of St Peter* by Guido Reni, an altarpiece on wood dating from 1605 commissioned by Cardinal Pietro Aldobrandini for the church of St Paul at the Tre Fontane; the *Martyrdom of St Erasmus* by Nicolas Poussin, an altarpiece completed in 1629 for the altar of the right transept of St Peter's Basilica in the Vatican; the *Communion of St Jerome* by Domenichino, oil on canvas for the Congregation of St Jerome of Charity of the church of the same name on Via Monserrato in Rome. Also present is the famous *Deposition from the Cross* by Caravaggio, considered one of the artist's finest masterpieces and among the main attractions in the Pinacoteca. Painted around 1604 as the altarpiece for the chapel of the Vittrice family in the church of St Mary in Vallicella (or *Chiesa Nuova*) in Rome, this canvas has long been studied, with its theme duplicated, by many painters.

Room XIII contains works by renowned 17th-century artists. These include Pietro da Cortona with *David killing Goliath* and *David killing the Lion*, oils on canvas from the collection of Cardinal Marcello Sacchetti. Also present are replicas of frescoes done for the cardinal's Villa del Pigneto by Pietro Berrettini between 1625 and 1630, and a work by Orazio Gentileschi, *Judith and her handmaid with the head of Holofernes*, also in oil on canvas. Of particular interest is an early work by Nicolas Poussin from 1625, the *Victory of Gideon over the Madianites*, an unusual theme in art history taken from the Book of Judges in the Old Testament. The canvas, from the Sacchetti collection, recalls the sudden night attack of the Jews on the Medianites, which the artist depicts with a mass of contorted bodies in various positions reminiscent of 16th-century battle scenes. The room also contains examples of Flemish portraiture such as the *Apotheosis of Vincenzo I Gonzaga* by the school of Rubens, and *St Ignatius of Loyola* by Antoine Van Dyck and his workshop, an altarpiece from 1623 showing the saint in adoration of Jesus' monogram, at his feet the armour he abandoned when he converted to become a soldier of Christ.

Room XIV contains Flemish and Italian floral painting. Many are the

Pinacoteca, Room IX, Leonardo da Vinci,
St Jerome
left and above, *St Jerome, details*

Pinacoteca, Room X, Titian,
Madonna with Child and Saints
left and above,
Madonna with Child and Saints, details

works in which flower garlands adorn sacred scenes and still lives; paintings in oil on canvas by such artists as Daniel Seghers, Erasmo II Quellinus, Franz Werner von Tamm, Andrea Belvedere and Pietro Navarra. Also present are religious portraits and themes dating from the 17th and 18th centuries, including the *Portrait of an Actor* by Pietro Paolini and the *Madonna and Child* by Sassoferrato, completed around 1650.

Room XV holds 18th-century paintings. The series *Astronomical Observations* is of particular importance within the panorama of European art. It was painted around 1711 by Donato Creti for Count Luigi Marsigli

Pinacoteca,
Room XI, Federico Barocci, Annunciation
left, *Room X, Veronese, Vision of St Helen*

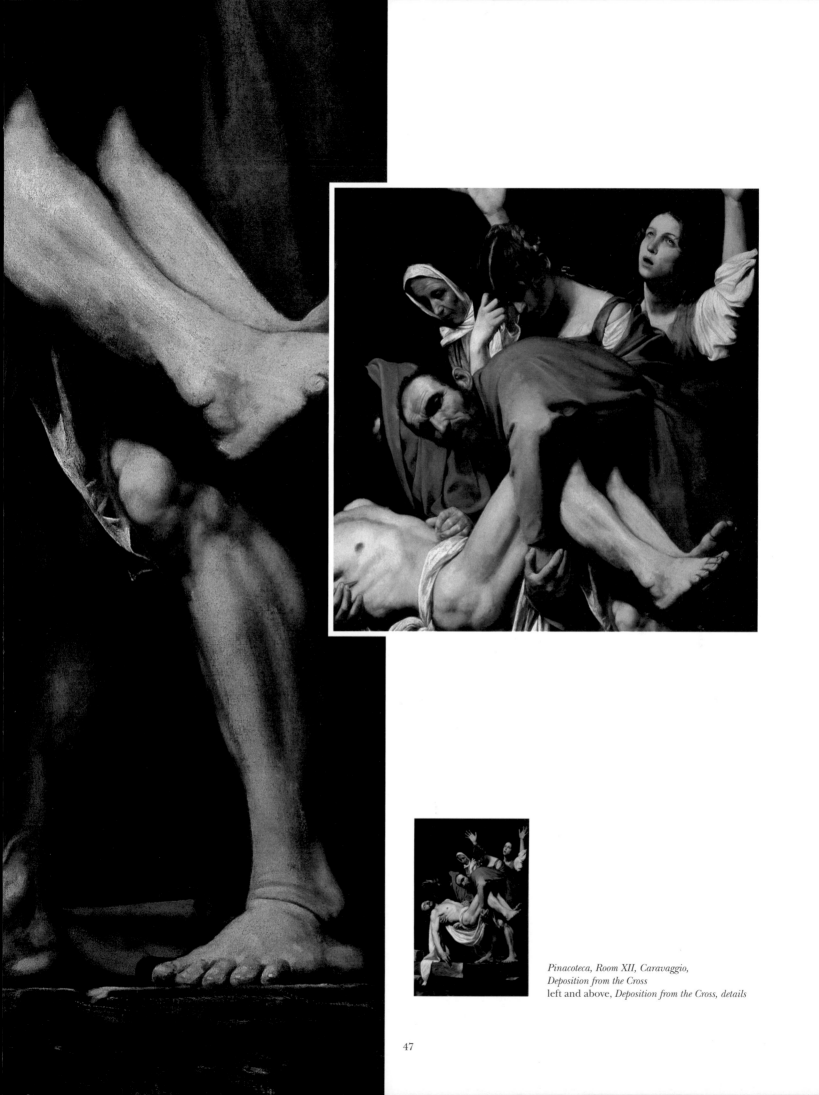

Pinacoteca, Room XII, Caravaggio,
Deposition from the Cross
left and above, *Deposition from the Cross, details*

who gave it as a gift to Pope Clement XI (1700-1721) in recognition for his having founded the Science Institute in Bologna, which included the first public observatory in Italy. The eight small oil canvases show tiny human figures, in a twilight scene, using telescopes and optical instruments to observe the planetary system as it was then known: the Sun, the Moon, Mercury, Venus, Mars, Jupiter, Saturn and a Comet. Alongside this series are important works by famous portraitists dating from the end of the 17th century to the beginning of the 19th. These include the *Portrait of George IV of England* that was commissioned in 1816 to the official painter of the British court, Thomas Lawrence, by the Prince Regent and future sovereign as a gift for Pope Pius VII, a sign of the climate of collaboration between the United Kingdom and the Holy See; the 1669 *Portrait of Clement IX* by Carlo Maratta from the Rospigliosi collection; and the *Portrait of Benedict XIV* by the Italian Giuseppe Maria Crespi. This work, of monumental proportions, was painted around 1740 by order of Cardinal Prospero Lambertini for the major seminary of Bologna. The artist later altered the vestments and added the papal tiara, after the cardinal archbishop of Bologna was elected pope, at which time the painting was also moved to Rome.

Room XVI is entirely dedicated to works by the famous Austrian painter, Wenzel Peter, who lived between the 18th and 19th centuries, and specialised in highly realistic depictions of nature. It is a unique collection in which the painter was able to use his profound zoological knowledge in depicting, with great artistic skill and scientific precision, over two hundred animals, each according to its specific characteristics: resting or moving or fighting. Among the works on display, all of the utmost significance, the big canvas *Adam and Eve in the Garden of Eden* and the *Fight between a lion and a tiger* are particularly outstanding. They were purchased by Gregory XVI (1831-1846) along with other works by the same artist to decorate the Consistory Hall in the Vatican Apostolic Palace.

Room XVII contains some of the preparatory models made by Gian Lorenzo Bernini and his workshop for the bronze statues of St Peter's Cathedra and the altar of the chapel of the Blessed Sacrament, works designed by the artist and located inside the Vatican Basilica. These models, life-size and of great documentary and artistic interest, were made in the second half of the 17th century by using a combination of clay, straw and wicker, with an iron framework fixed on a wooden base. They were used to make the moulds in which the definitive bronze statues were then cast. From the great cathedra at the centre of the

Pinacoteca, Room XIII, Nicolas Poussin, Victory of Gideon over the Madianites

apse - a marble, stucco and gilded bronze structure holding the precious Carolingian wooden and ivory throne - we have four full-length *Angels* and two *Doctors of the Church*: St Athanasius and St John Chrysostom. From the altar of the chapel of the Blessed Sacrament, we have the model for the *Kneeling Angel* to the right of the tabernacle. The model for the angel on the left is kept in the Artistic Historical Museum (Treasury of St Peter's) in the Vatican.

Room XVIII, the last room of the Vatican Pinacoteca, contains the collection of Byzantine icons; an important artistic heritage accumulated through donations, legacies, grants and purchases. There are over a hundred works in tempera on wood dating from the 15th to the 19th

Pinacoteca, Room XV,
Thomas Lawrence, Portrait of George IV of England
left, *Carlo Maratta, Portrait of Clement IX*

centuries, for the most part from the Slavic and Greek worlds, with some from the West. Among the oldest works in the Vatican collection is the 15th-century *Madonna of the Milk* by the Cretan painter Antonio Papadopoulos, and a tempera with oil glazing from Russia – probably by the Novgorod school – showing *St Nicholas and events from his life*. This icon, which can be dated to the end of the 15th century, shows the figure of the saint conferring a blessing, framed by sixteen episodes from his life, from his early years to the miracles done in adulthood as bishop. All the stories belong to hagiographic and popular tradition: saving of shipwrecked sailors, healing a possessed person, finding of the lost child, St Nicholas staying the executioners hand as he is about to decapitate three officers, St Nicholas appearing to Emperor Constantine in a dream.

Pinacoteca,
Room XVII, Gian Lorenzo Bernini, left Angel,
preparatory model for the bronze statue of St Peter's Cathedra
right, Room XVIII, Russian Art (Novgorod?), St Nicholas and events from his life
pages 52 and 53, Room XVI, Wenzel Peter, Fight of a lion with a tiger, detail

GREGORIAN EGYPTIAN MUSEUM

Ancient Egypt, according to sacred Scripture, has a fundamental importance in the history of human salvation. Hence, perhaps, the interest of some popes in that civilisation. In Egypt, moreover, lie the origins of the artistic language that, through the flowering and maturity of Greek art, subsequently led to the creation of modern figurative western art. The Gregorian Egyptian Museum, then, has an essential role in recording this fascinating and still mysterious world.

In ancient Egypt, artistic representation was closely associated with the exercise of political power. It was a way of considering art and communication among men that inevitably led to forms of collective creativity.

The repetitive nature of the figurative canon was fundamental to the historical foundation of power. This canon included idealisation of form, reduction and two-dimensional vision. Depictions of the human body concentrated on the elements that best served to represent it, hence the characteristic portrayal of both profile (face and limbs) and front (eyes and torso) in the same view. It presents a depiction of reality that contained no attempt to reflect nature. The problem of rendering perspective and the three dimensions was common to both painting and reliefs. The fact that in ancient Egypt writing in ideograms appeared alongside these images meant that the unchangeable forms were associated to a form of communication linked to the exercise of political power.

The Egyptian Museum, an initiative of the Barnabite Egyptologist Fr. Luigi Maria Ungarelli, was inaugurated on 2nd February 1839, the eighth anniversary of the election to the papal throne of Gregory XVI (1831-1846). It is housed in the Belvedere Palace of Innocent VIII and contains antiquities and monuments of ancient Egypt, many of them found in Rome and at Villa Adriana in Tivoli. The nucleus of the collection was also formed through the acquisition of 19th century private collections.

The museum is divided into nine rooms, the fifth of which - the so called "hemicycle" - overlooks the first floor terrace of the Niche of the Pigna. A complete renovation of the museum in 1989 did not alter its typically 19th-century exhibition structure.

Room I contains an epigraphic collection of statues and steles with hieroglyphic inscriptions. The architecture of the hall itself reflects the Egyptian style. Among the exhibits is a statue of *Ramses II* on his throne and the headless statue of *Oudjahorresne*, priest and physician at the service of the pharaohs of the Saitic dynasty.

Room II contains ancient Egyptian funerary objects. It also has a long, painted inscription in hieroglyphics extolling the founder of the museum, Gregory XVI: "His Majesty, the supreme Pontiff, the munificent Gregory, sovereign and father of Christian mankind of all countries, in order to make the city of Rome shine with his bounty, took the

Gregorian Egyptian Museum, Room I,
Scarab
left, *Statue of Oudjahorresne*
page 56 and 57, *View of Room III, in the foreground statue of Osiris-Antinous*

largest and most beautiful figures of ancient Egypt and made this place...".

The next room houses a reconstruction of the *Serapeum* and the *Canopus,* an architectural complex at Villa Adriana in Tivoli. It is a re-creation of the geography of ancient Egypt with a long corridor representing the valley of the Nile, and a great semicircle symbolizing the delta of that river. Other exhibits worthy of note include the colossal torso of *Isis-Demeter* and four white marble statues portraying *Osiris-Antinous,* sculptured in memory of the boy Antinous from Bithynia who died during the flood of the Nile in 130 AD.

The influence of Egyptian art on Roman forms is evident in the statues exhibited in Room IV. These are Egyptian-like figures, interpreted according to the classical taste and language of Roman art, for example a large black marble sculpture from the 2nd century portrays the river *Nile.*

Room V, the so-called "hemicycle", holds monumental sculptures of divinities and pharaohs dating from between 2000 BC and 200 AD.

The next small room, Room VI, contains various bronze objects used in worship: *ex voto,* protective amulets and various cult objects testifying to the popular religious traditions.

Room VII houses exhibits donated by the Orientalist Carlo Grassi in 1952. An inscription on the wall recalls the donation of this collection, which is made up of a broad series of small bronzes and clay figures from Greco-Roman Egypt.

Room VIII contains archaeological finds from Mesopotamia and Syria-Palestine dating from before the Classical Age.

The last room, Room IX, is dedicated to Assyrian reliefs from the royal palaces built in Mesopotamia at the time of the expansion of the Persian Empire into Egypt and the Mediterranean.

PIO-CLEMENTINO MUSEUM

orange trees and the famous statue collection of Julius II. The addition of a portico doubled the number of sides, reduced the central open space, and the courtyard was transformed into the present Octagonal Courtyard.

Although Pope Clement XIV undertook many important initiatives, he had neither the fortitude nor the intention to completely modify the original plan of the *Palazzetto.* This was left to his successor, Pius VI (Angelo Braschi 1775-1799) who ordered the destruction of the famous chapel frescoed by Mantegna in order to give organic unity to the Statue Gallery. Pope Pius also created a series of great exhibition halls and, above all, had the entrance relocated, thus inverting the museum route. Indeed, by entering the museum not through the *Corridore della Libraria* but through the Simonetti Staircase, located on the opposite side, meant that access was no longer from the pontifical apartments but from an entrance built exclusively for the public. In this way, Pope Clement XIV's intention of making the collections public to guarantee their permanence was realized by his successor through the museum structure itself, which was "turned to face" the public. On Simonetti's death, the work was completed by Giuseppe Camporese who, by order of the pope, designed

In 1771, Pope Clement XIV (Giovanni Vincenzo Ganganelli 1769-1774) established a museum in what was then the *Palazzetto del Belvedere.* The Palazzetto had been built for Innocent VIII (1484-1492) by Jacopo da Pietrasanta according to a design by Antonio del Pollaiolo, and had, since the pontificate of Julius II (1503-1513), housed the Statue Antiquarium. Pope Clement's aim was to rescue works of art from oblivion and, following an incisive acquisition policy to secure certain masterpieces from antique dealers and foreign collectors, found he needed a suitable place to keep his new purchases. He wanted to add them to other works already in Vatican possession and to those being discovered during excavations undertaken by the Papal States at that time. He therefore commissioned architect Alessandro Dori to create a space suitable for holding the collections of classical antiquities, which popes had been adding to since Renaissance times. Dori died a year after work began and was replaced by Michelangelo Simonetti, the architect of the Apostolic Palace. The alterations he made turned the old apartments of Pope Innocent into a museum and gave a new look to the internal courtyard of the Palace. This courtyard, known as the "Courtyard of the Statues", was originally square and filled with

a new entrance leading to the famous Staircase: the Atrium of the Four Gates. Still today the inscriptions *Museum Clementinum* and *Museum Pium*, placed respectively over the internal doors of the Square Vestibule and of the Hall of the Greek Cross, indicate the different solutions chosen by the two pontiffs.

The public nature of the collections is not the only novelty of the Pio-Clementino. The museum also represents an important change in the way exhibition areas were conceived. For the first time ever these areas were structured around the collections, with the creation of a "container" that was classically inspired because it was to hold ancient art. The rooms were designed by the architects in accordance with the dictates of Pius VI. However, they clearly follow the wishes of Giovanni Battista Visconti, then director of the Museum. They make a direct reference to certain Roman buildings: for example, the *Sala Rotonda*, a reinterpretation of the Pantheon's coffered dome with central oculus, and the Hall of the Greek Cross, which draws its inspiration from rooms in Roman baths. The decorations are also derived from the ancient world. It suffices to mention the ceiling of the Hall of the Muses or that of the Mask Room, decorated with scenes from classical mythology. Simple imitation can become novel usage where, for example, a Roman mosaic taken from the Otricoli Baths is set in the floor of the *Sala Rotonda* or the door of the Hall of the Greek Cross is embellished with two telamons that are examples of the Egyptian-like tastes during the era of Hadrian. They were taken from Villa Adriana in Tivoli.

A visit to the museum, bearing in mind that the route is once again that envisaged by Clement XIV, starts from the Square Vestibule. In a niche on the left is the *sarcophagus of Lucius Cornelius Scipio Barbato*, consul in 298 BC. It shows Hellenistic influences and was taken from the tomb of the Scipioni on the Via Appia.

Across the Round Vestibule is the *Gabinetto of Apoxyomenos* containing the sculpture bearing that name, a 1st-century Roman marble copy of a bronze statue from about 320 BC. The original by Lysippos is mentioned by Pliny the

Pio-Clementino Museum,
Octagonal Courtyard, Apollo Belvedere

Elder in his *Naturalis Historia*. It shows the athlete in the moment following his exertions, when physical effort and even the glory of victory are mitigated in the act of wiping the body. The heroic dimension thus gives way to the human one, both physical and psychological. It is an important shift in the language of ancient art and an extraordinarily modern choice towards depicting man naturally, capturing him in a moment of everyday life. To solve the problem of the figure in space, Lysippos used a solution which his contemporaries must have considered audacious. The dynamism of the outstretched arm decisively breaks the frontal view, bringing the gesture to penetrate into space. The extremely balanced structure, the figure which stretches in almost linear tension, the light body and the tiny head enable us to recognise Lysippos as a transitional artist between the Classical and the Hellenistic periods. The statue was discovered in 1849 in Trastevere at the Vicolo delle Palme, since renamed Vicolo dell'Atleta, and was restored by the sculptor Pietro Tenerani (1789-1869). The work aroused great interest all over Europe and numerous copies were made. After being moved several times between the *Gabinetto dell'Hermes* in the Octagonal Courtyard and the Braccio Nuovo, the sculpture was placed in its current location in 1932.

The Octagonal Courtyard contains the original nucleus of Julius II's collection, including some of the most important works of the Vatican Museums. In four of the corners are the four *Gabinetti* of Apollo, Laocoon, Hermes and Canova.

The *Apollo Belvedere*, originally in the church of St Peter in Chains, Julius' titular church when he was a cardinal, has been in its present site since 1509. It is a 2nd-century AD Roman copy of a 4th-century BC bronze original attributed to the sculptor Leochares. It shows the naked god in steady pose and armed with a bow, emblem and tool of his avenging power. The statue's forearms and arms were added in 1532 by Giovanni Angelo da Montorsoli. They were removed in 1924 and put back in 1999. The work was considered a Greek original until the end of the 18th century when the Parthenon reliefs were found and it was identified as a Roman copy, reducing its renown though not its charm. The great purity and nobility of the gods is represented in this form of mysterious lightness where avenging power becomes a painless act, an expression of splendour, a play of style. The great fascination of the *Apollo Belvedere* has touched distant intellectual horizons, inserting itself into apparently remote areas of art: consider the metaphysical nature of Giorgio De Chirico's *Chant d'amour*, where the head of Apollo appears beside a kitchen glove.

Pio-Clementino Museum, Octagonal Courtyard,
group of Laocoon, detail
left, *group of Laocoon*

In the *Gabinetto of Laocoon* is the marble group of that name. Discovered in 1506 near the *Domus Aurea* it is, according to Pliny the Elder in his *Naturalis Historia*, the work of a group of sculptors from Rhodes: Hagesandros, Athanodoros and Polydoros. Michelangelo and Giuliano da Sangallo were present at its discovery and advised Pope Julius II to buy it. Disinterred after its long burial, the sculpture was extensively damaged and required much restoration and repair - undertaken by Montorsoli using earthenware - which returned the group to its original unity, though sacrificing any certainty as to its original form. Its present state is the result of a restoration by Filippo Magi between 1957 and 1960. This marvellous work of art shows the priest of Apollo as he dies with his sons in the toils of two marine serpents sent by the goddess Athena. She had been angered at his opposition to allowing the wooden horse to enter Troy. The plastic energy - expressed in the tension of the bodies and the faces, in the "serpents that make Laocoon lament" (the phrase is Pietro Aretino's) - conveys a sense of restrained tragedy, the impending drama suspended in a moment of measured anguish. The agony of the bodies tormented by the terrible divine penalty may be inter-

CVRA · PII · VII ·

preted as a metaphor of the derision and pain to which all bearers of truth are condemned.

The *Gabinetto of Hermes* contains the statue of that name. It is a Roman copy from the age of Hadrian of a 4th-century BC Greek bronze. It was discovered near Castel Sant'Angelo in 1543 during the pontificate of Pope Paul III. Because it was discovered near Emperor Hadrian's mausoleum, the statue was at first wrongly identified as being Antinous, Hadrian's favourite. However Hermes, the messenger of the gods, is identifiable by his travel mantle and by his depiction as *psychopompos*, i.e. guide to the souls of the dead in the pagan afterlife.

Further down the Courtyard is one of the most famous and admired statues, the *Venus Felix*, probably discovered near the Roman basilica of Santa Croce in Gerusalemme and part of Julius II's collection at least since 1509. The pose of the sculpture is inspired by the famous Aphrodite of Knidos by Praxiteles, and shows either Faustina the Younger, wife of Emperor Marcus Aurelius, Crispina, wife of Commodus, or a less-known Roman matron who, in any case, lived in the second half of the 2nd century AD. One of the woman's sons, depicted as Eros, stands beside her.

The *Gabinetto* of Canova contains three statues commissioned from that artist by Pius VII (1800-1823) around 1800 to replace the sculptures seized by Napoleon's troops. The first shows *Perseus Triumphant* with Pluto's helmet, Vulcan's sword and Mercury's sandals, holding the

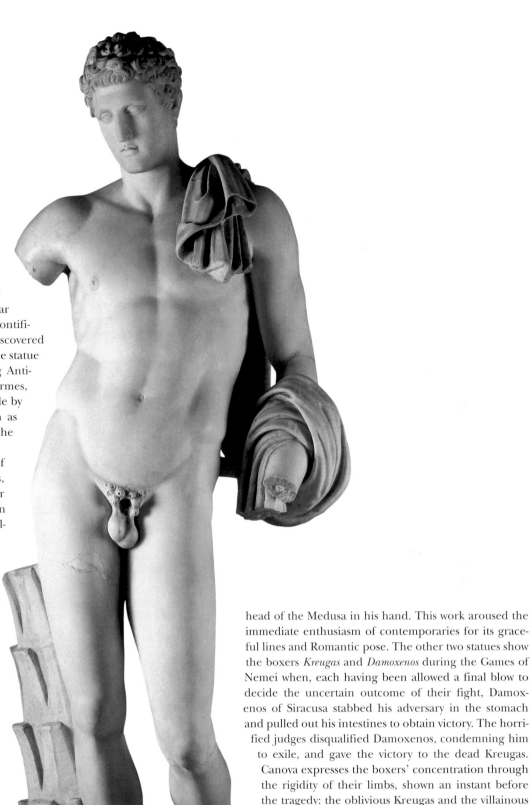

Pio-Clementino Museum, Octagonal Courtyard,
Hermes
left, *Antonio Canova,*
Perseus Triumphant

head of the Medusa in his hand. This work aroused the immediate enthusiasm of contemporaries for its graceful lines and Romantic pose. The other two statues show the boxers *Kreugas* and *Damoxenos* during the Games of Nemei when, each having been allowed a final blow to decide the uncertain outcome of their fight, Damoxenos of Siracusa stabbed his adversary in the stomach and pulled out his intestines to obtain victory. The horrified judges disqualified Damoxenos, condemning him to exile, and gave the victory to the dead Kreugas. Canova expresses the boxers' concentration through the rigidity of their limbs, shown an instant before the tragedy: the oblivious Kreugas and the villainous Damoxenos are protagonists in a sudden act of fatal dramatic power.

The Octagonal Courtyard leads through to a series of spaces containing works arranged according to a similar genre or a common subject.

The Animal Room is so-called for the many fragments of ancient sculptures of animals, much restored by Francesco Antonio Franzoni. There is a beautiful copy from the Anto-

Pio-Clementino Museum, Animal Room,
view of the Room
above, *Leopard*

Pio-Clementino Museum, Gallery of Statues,
view of the Gallery
above, *Apollo Sauroktonos*

nine Age of a bronze work by Scopas from the 4th century BC showing *Meleager* with his dog and the head of a wild boar of Calydonian, which he killed and gave to his beloved Atalanta.

The Gallery of Statues contains, among other works, a Roman copy of a bronze by Praxiteles from around 360 BC, the *Apollo Sauroktonos* ("lizard-killer"). It is a fine depiction of the young god an instant before he kills, using a small arrow, a lizard resting on a tree trunk. This very high-quality copy well renders the vague sinuosity of Praxiteles' works. The languid, almost voluptuous charm of the relaxed Apollo inculcates a terrible sense of dread for the impending cruel act. The profound and gloomy meditations of ancient art give way to light distraction, to a delicate but cruel game. The next room, the Gallery of Busts, contains a huge quantity of Roman busts. On the other hand, the Mask Room, situated in an avant-corps of the Belvedere Palace, owes its name to the floor mosaic depicting ancient theatrical masks. The mosaic dates from the 2nd century AD and was taken from Villa Adriana in Tivoli. This small room contains Roman copies of some of the most famous Greek classical statues. Among them are a Roman copy of a Hellenistic original representing the *Three Graces*, a work which inspired Canova, and a *Venus of Knidos*, based on the bronze original by Praxiteles. The latter is one of the first classical works to depict the female nude. The goddess is shown immediately after removing her clothes before her bath; her serene imperturbability is emphasised by her natural, intimate gestures.

The famous *Belvedere Torso* stands in the centre of the so-called Hall of the Muses, built by Simonetti in 1780. Its ceiling frescoes are by Tommaso Conca. The hall also contains marble statues of *Apollo and the Muses*, found near Tivoli in 1775 during the excavation of a Roman villa. The Torso has been repeatedly identified as Hercules, above all for the skin on which the majestic figure is sitting. Others have suggested Marsyas, Polyphemus or Philoctetes, but the doubt as to the exact identity has never been resolved. A signature on the base identifies it as the work of "Apollonius, son of Nestor, Athenian". It was greatly admired by Renaissance masters once Michelangelo recognised the energy in its

Pio-Clementino Museum,
Room of Masks, Belvedere Torso
left, *view of the Room of Masks*

Pio-Clementino Museum, Round Room,
view of the Room
above, *detail of the floor*

79

MVSEVM · PIVM

plastic vigour. It was, as may be seen by a quick comparison with the "Ignudi" of the Sistine Chapel, one of the works that inspired that famous artist, and is considered as the starting point of his modernity.

A monumental monolithic porphyry basin, found in the *Domus Aurea* and measuring 13 metres in circumference, stands in the centre of the *Sala Rotonda*. The room's wall niches hold a series of statues, some of them direct expressions of Roman sculpture, others copies of Greek works.

The last room is the Hall of the Greek Cross, so called because of its shape. It is characterized by two shining examples of late-ancient art, the majestic porphyry *sarcophagi of Constance and Helen*, respectively daughter and mother of Emperor Constantine. The former comes from the Mausoleum of Constance on the Via Nomentana and dates from 350-360 AD. It is decorated with reliefs of small figures harvesting grapes, a Christian symbol of life. The latter, dating from the early 4th century AD, comes from Helen's Mausoleum on the Via Labicana and is decorated with scenes of Roman knights triumphing over the barbarians.

Pio-Clementino Museum, view of the Greek-Cross Room

CHARIOT ROOM

The concept and creation of this Room belong to the creative genius of Giuseppe Camporese, a pupil of Pasquale Belli and a member of an important family of Italian architects working in Rome and Lazio. With his father and brother he completed the dome of the church of St Andrew in Subiaco, and with his brother he built the church of St Thomas at Villanova in Genzano and the Pius VI Hall of the Germanic College in Rome. He also built the chapel of St Stephen of the Hungarians in the Roman church of Santo Stefano Rotondo.

He was appointed pontifical architect at the age of 32 as collaborator to Michelangelo Simonetti and, at the latter's death in 1787, became architect to Pope Pius VI (1775-1799). Camporese showed a more academic taste than Simonetti, which he expressed with a meticulous analysis of classical models reinterpreted through the study of 16th-century architecture.

It was in this fervent artistic environment that, in 1786, Camporese planned the Atrium of the Four Gates, which later became the entrance to the Vatican Museums. His plan involved the creation of an upper room, but this was only completed in 1794 when the floor was laid. This upper room, near the Gallery of Candelabra, is the Chariot Room, a circular hall with walls completely covered in Carrara marble and with four large pilasters alternating with arched recesses. The pilasters contain niches with classical-style statues and, at the ends, fluted semi-columns cabled to a third of their height, resting on high plinths and topped with Corinthian capitals. The recesses have windows. The polychrome marble floor has elements of the Braschi coat-of-arms, and the dome, resting on an entablature that runs all the way round the hall, has octagonal coffering and a central oculus whence the light enters and falls on the great chariot in the middle of the room.

The massive marble group is the work of Francesco Antonio Franzoni, who used as the body of the chariot an old triumphal carriage dating from the 1st century AD which, decorated with volutes and flowers of acanthus in bas-relief, had previously been used as an episcopal chair in the Roman church of St Mark. Franzoni's contribution - a typical example of 18th-century usage of ancient objects - was limited to attaching the wheels, the shaft and one of the horses, the torso of which was donated by Prince Borghese. The group has been placed on a rectangular basement protected by a wooden balustrade.

Around the walls of the room are Roman sculptures, including a statue of *Dionysius*, identified as *Sardanapalos* from the inscription on the edge of the mantle, which is a Roman imperial copy of a Greek original by an artist from the circle of Praxiteles (late 4th century BC); *five sarcophagi of children* from the 2nd-3rd century AD decorated with bas-reliefs of chariot races of cupids at the circus, an emblem of the struggle for life; and a statue of *Discobulus preparing to throw*, a copy from the early-imperial age of an original by a sculptor belonging to the school of Polycleitos.

The athlete is portrayed just before the throw, his whole body tense with concentration. Finally there is a statue of *Discobolus throwing the discus*, a Roman copy from the time of Hadrian (2nd century AD) from a bronze original by Myron (ca. 460 BC) from Villa Adriana in Tivoli. Here the artist has managed to capture the athlete's inner feelings and intense absorption as he is about to throw.

CHIARAMONTI MUSEUM

GALLERY OF INSCRIPTIONS

BRACCIO NUOVO

The Chiaramonti Museum, named after its founder Pius VII (Gregorio Chiaramonti 1800-1823), was created between 1805 and 1807. It is a museum of ancient sculptures assembled under the direction of Antonio Canova (then Inspector General of Fine Arts) in the gallery originally named *Corridore della Libraria*, designed by Bramante to link the Pontifical Palace to the Belvedere Palace. It holds a thousand ancient sculptures discovered during excavations or acquired from private collections. Apart from a few changes, the museum follows Canova's arrangement.

At first, the exhibition seems a bit monotonous, with objects displayed along the entire length of the walls following a rigid scheme in which groups of three statues alternate with sectors containing fragments of sarcophagi, portraits on shelves and reliefs. In fact, this choice was dictated by historical reasons. The difficulties faced by the papacy during the Napoleonic age, when the French requisitioned many works of art, made it impossible to create a lavish exhibition area using precious materials, as had been the case some decades before with the Pio-Clementino Museum. Indeed the only indulgence, in deep contrast to the bare walls, is the re-use of ancient cornices as shelves for busts. Despite many difficulties, Pius VII wanted to assert papal authority, and succeeded in doing so by exhibiting such an enormous number of works, which seem even more than they actually are due to the flat way in which they are arranged. Moreover, the repetitiveness of the Chiaramonti Museum also had an educational aim as Pius VII's museum became one of the main tools for the study of portraiture, which in that period was developing towards modernity. Among the many artworks in the gallery are the following:

- The *funerary monument to Publius Nonius Zethus*, a miller and flour trader who lived in the 1st century AD.
- The *funerary statue of Cornuto*, a late-imperial Roman work (end 3rd century AD). The subject is identified in the inscription: "Here am I, Cornuto, sorrowful with my eight beloved children". Cornuto is depicted as Saturn, enthroned with a sickle in his hand and surrounded by children.
- A sculpture group from the 2nd century AD depicting the *Shepherd Ganymedes*, famous for his beauty, *with the eagle* sent by Zeus to abduct him so he could become cupbearer to the gods.
- A majestic *Head of Athena*, a Roman copy dating from the age of Hadrian, probably from the original of Athena Pròmachos by Phidias (5th century BC).
- A relief representing the *Three Graces*, a copy from the late 1st century BC, probably from a Greek original of 470 BC which was in the

Propylaeum of the Acropolis in Athens.
- A small statue of *Ulysses* depicted in the act of offering drink to Polyphemus. The work, dating from the 1st century AD, was inspired by Greek models and originally belonged to a group that told the story of the Cyclops.

A gate divides the Chiaramonti Museum from the Gallery of Inscriptions, which occupies the first part of Bramante's Corridor. It houses one of the world's most important collections of Latin and Greek inscriptions (over three thousand fragments), both pagan and Christian, arranged and classified by Gaetano Marini (1740-1815). The collection provides an endless source for the study of ancient epigraphy. It was started under the pontificate of Benedict XIV (1740-1758) and grew considerably under Clement XIV (1769-1774), Pius VI (1775-1799) and under the personal supervision of Pius VII himself.

Perpendicular to the Chiaramonti Museum is the Braccio Nuovo (New Wing), a museum of classical sculpture planned and ordered by Pius VII in 1806 but, due to the problems of the French occupation, only completed between 1817 and 1822 to a design by Raffaele Stern. Its name reveals its association with Pius VII's first museum; it is, in fact, the "New Wing of the Chiaramonti Museum". The old and the new structures respectively constitute the eastern and southern sides of the Courtyard of the Pigna, which is closed on its north and west sides by the Belvedere Palace and by the Galleries of the Vatican Apostolic Library. Unlike the previous museum, which was created within a pre-existing building, this time the pope ordered a completely new exhibition area, as Pius VI had earlier done with the rooms of the Pio-Clementino Museum. This neo-classical building has a long gallery opening onto a central hemicycle with a coffered barrel vault, and illuminated by a series of skylights creating an effect of light diffused from above. The internal walls have niches containing statues interspersed with numerous busts, while above is a series of stucco bas-reliefs by Francesco Massimiliano Laboureur. The structure uses columns taken from other buildings, while the floors are covered with re-used mosaics: beautiful black and white works dating from the 2nd century AD, from the excavations at Tor Marancia on the Via

Chiaramonti Museum, Ganymedes and the eagle
pages 84 and 85, *view of the Braccio Nuovo*

Ardeatina. The only coloured mosaic, located in the hemicycle, shows the *Artemis of Ephesus*. It was made a few years earlier for the rooms of the Quirinal Palace and re-used here.

The Braccio Nuovo houses some absolute masterpieces of classical art, arranged thematically like the works in the Pio-Clementino: the section nearer the Chiaramonti contains works on the theme of Roman history, the other section on the theme of Greek mythology. Among the most famous works is the so-called *Augustus of Prima Porta*, a statue of a figure wearing a breastplate found in 1863 in the villa of Livia, Augustus's wife, on the Via Flaminia. It is a marble copy, probably made for the widow a year after Augustus' death (14 AD). It was inspired by a bronze original which celebrates - as may be seen from the bas-reliefs on the cuirass - the return of the Roman military insignia lost by Crassus in 53 BC and the conciliatory policies pursued by the emperor. Augustus is shown in the *adlocutio* gesture, that is with his right hand raised while addressing his troops. His bare feet are a reference to his divine dignity, while Cupid riding a dolphin on the base of the statue refers to Venus, progenitrix of the *gens Julia* and celestial ancestress of Augustus. The posture is that of the *Doryphorus* by Polycleitos.

The *Statue of the Nile* in the centre of the gallery was presumably discovered in 1513 near the Roman church of Santa Maria Sopra Minerva. It is probably a 1st-century AD copy of a Hellenistic original. The personification of the river deity is characterized by the presence of crocodiles and sphinxes, and of sixteen boys alluding to the river's fertility.

The Roman copy of the *Doryphorus* (literally "spear carrier"), also in the Braccio Nuovo, is one of many replicas of Polycleitos' 440-BC masterpiece. This is one of the most important works of antiquity, representing perhaps Achilles with his spear, defined also as the *kanon* (canon) for the proportions of the body as theorized by the sculptor Polycleitos and represented here. During Roman times and afterwards the statue was considered an example of the perfect representation of the human figure. The scheme used is the so-called "chiastic", which reproduces the chiasm, the Greek letter χ. This is clear from the position of the upper and lower limbs positioned in a cross. Looking at the statue in profile, one can see the contrast between the forward gesture of the left arm and of the right leg, in perfect balance. The archetype Greek ideal expressed in this figure of limpid and serene elegance was, until the Baroque, a model for anatomical representation in portraits and full-length sculptures.

Braccio Nuovo, Augustus of Prima Porta

MVNIF.PII.IX.P.M.

GREGORIAN ETRUSCAN MUSEUM

The Etruscan civilisation, with its city-states, long dominated central Italy before it was finally overcome by the Romans. The Etruscan contribution to what we now call western culture was essential, indeed the real level of that contribution is much greater than is recognised today. Although the norms of art and law, the principles of European civilisation, may be traced back to Greek and Roman culture, the fundamental role played by the Etruscans (called "Thyrrenes" by the Greek historian Herodotus) in these areas is often disregarded. The Romans founded their empire by assimilating and absorbing the cultural traits of the peoples they conquered, thus enriching their own cultural heritage. Roman art was also influenced by the Etruscans. A good and highly symbolic example is the famous bronze Capitoline She-wolf, symbol of Rome, housed in the Capitoline Museums. It is an Etruscan work to which the twins were added later.

Etruscan figurative art is characterised not only by the influence of Greek models but also by a style clearly inspired in the concepts of religion and work. It is not limited then, as is often wrongly believed, to the cult of the dead, though most of the archaeological finds do refer to this cult.

The collection of Etruscan antiquities in the Vatican Museums is housed in a museum founded by Gregory XVI (1831-1846) and inaugurated on 2nd February 1837, the sixth anniversary of his election to the papal throne. The motivation behind the creation of the museum lay in the growth of research and study of Etruscan civilisation, above all in southern Etruria, in the first half of the 19th century. The great excavations, whence came most of the objects and furnishings of the museum, marked the beginning of an acquisition policy. The main excavation for this collection was done in 1836-1837 in the necropolis of Sorbo (south of Cerveteri).

Room I of the museum has a collection of sarcophagi, reliefs and urns, some made of local stone and others ascribable to Villanovan culture, so-called for the place near Bologna where they were

Gregorian Etruscan Museum,
Room XIX, Exekias, amphora portraying Achilles and Ajax
pages 88 and 89, *View of Room IV*

found in 1853. The objects are from the early Iron Age in Etruria and Lazio, and from the East. Among them we may mention the characteristic bi-conical funerary urns with their complex geometric decorations.

Room II, with frescoes by Barocci and by Federico and Taddeo Zuccari, contains the most important nucleus of the collection found in the necropolis of Sorbo. This includes the *Regolini-Galassi* Tomb (from the names of the discoverers): a three-room tomb with a very rich collection of gold jewellery and silver vases. Noteworthy objects include a circular *gold fibula* decorated with geometric vegetal and animal motifs, and a chariot. The tomb was intended to accommodate two people of princely rank: a woman and, presumably, a warrior.

Room III is decorated with 16th-century frescoes depicting scenes from the Old Testament and houses a collection of bronzes. In the centre of the room is a bronze statue, the so-called *Mars of Todi*, a rare example of an Italic statue that portrays a young man wearing a breastplate in the act of offering wine to the divinity. The work shows clear influences of 5th-century BC Greek art. The room also contains the so-called *Putto of Carrara*, an *ex voto* portraying a young boy in the act of making an offering to the divinity.

Room IV contains sarcophagi, urns and reliefs, sculpted in the local tufa, *nenfro*, readily available in southern Etruria and particularly appreciated by local sculptors for its softness and malleability. These works, which largely seem to follow the customs of archaic art, must originally have been stuccoed with rich polychromes, now lost. Particularly noteworthy are two lions from Vulci dating from the 6th century BC.

Further along is the Guglielmi Room containing the collection of Benedetto Guglielmi. Part of it was donated to Pope Pius XI in 1937, while the remaining part remained in the hands of Guglielmi's heirs until 1987, when it was purchased by the Vatican Museums.

The collection contains Etruscan and Greek ceramics and bronzes, as well as objects in gold testifying to the very high levels of skill attained by Etruscan goldsmiths in working this material.

The next Rooms contain important examples of Etruscan cinerary urns sculpted in natural stone. Cremation rites were widespread, mainly in northern Etruria. These particular works shows how Greek myths existed alongside the depiction of local myths.

The Gregorian Etruscan Museum also houses an *Antiquarium Romanum*, an abundant collection of Roman antiquities, mostly fragments of minor arts from Rome and Lazio, including parts of statues, furniture, pots and polychrome glass objects. The final rooms contain a collection of vases unearthed during 19th-century excavations. Attic ceramic painting is much in evidence on finds of Greek origin. Ceramics were very popular in Etruria, and the numerous commercial exchanges between Greeks and Etruscans are confirmed by the evident influences to which Etruscan art was subject and also by the discovery of Greek originals in Etruscan areas. Among the masterpieces here displayed is an Attic amphora with black figures showing *Achilles and Ajax playing draughts*, executed by the painter and vase-maker Exekias in about 530 BC. The episode depicted does not belong to Homeric tradition. The two characters are portrayed with great skill, and with a certain gravity that is typical of Exekias' art.

Gregorian Etruscan Museum, Room III, Mars of Todi

Gregorian Etruscan Museum,
Room XI, Funerary monument with dying Adonis
above, *Room II, gold fibula*

UPPER GALLERIES

On the upper floor of the Vatican Palaces, along the west wing overlooking the Belvedere Courtyard, is a sequence of three galleries. In the history of art collection and the evolution of spaces dedicated to the display of art, the gallery reflects a move away from humanistic introspection (well represented by the "private space" of the small studio) and towards a late-Renaissance taste for exhibition. This took concrete form in the creation of public and "representational" areas by artistic patrons as an act of self-glorification. In Italy, galleries came into being around the mid 16th century and the first to be built in the Vatican Apostolic Palace was the Gallery of Maps.

The Gallery of Maps is a vital historical record of the level of academic study of geography and cartography at the time of the Bolognese Pope Gregory XIII (Ugo Boncompagni 1572-1585). The work of Ottaviano Mascherino, who became palace architect in 1577, the gallery was built between 1578 and 1580 by adding a floor to the west wing of the Belvedere Courtyard. It consists of a corridor 120 m long and 6 m wide, divided into seventeen bays with sixteen rectangular windows on each side and, in the middle, an opening overlooking a balcony. Its huge dimensions and the natural light coming from openings on both walls make it resemble French galleries.

The floor is of dichromate marble with geometrical motifs, while the intradoses of the windows are completely frescoed with grotesques. The barrel vault covering the gallery is richly decorated with stuccos and paintings designed by Girolamo Muziano and executed by Cesare Nebbia and other artists, including Antonio Tempesta, Lorenzo Sabbatini, Niccolò Circignani delle Pomarance and Jacopo Sementa. Within a series of geometric divisions are episodes from the *Acts of the Apostles*, scenes from the life of *John the Baptist, Sts Benedict, Bernardino, Romuald* and *Peter Damian, Popes Sylvester I, Leo the Great* and *Celestine V*, as well as allegories, landscapes, arabesques and twenty-four episodes from the Old Testament, painted in monochrome. The stucco cornices of the vault, with broken tympanums upon which rest nudes, recall the Roman galleries of Palazzo Capodiferro-Spada and Palazzo Farnese. The frescoed scenes, as indicated by the inscriptions - are associated with the territories painted on the gallery walls between the windows. They total forty maps depicting the whole of Italy, single regions, islands and Church estates.

Gallery of Maps,
Ignazio Danti, Plan of the Isle of Malta, detail
left, *Ignazio Danti, Plan of ancient Italy*
pages 94 and 95, *view of the Gallery*

These paintings were commissioned by Gregory XIII from the Dominican friar Ignazio Danti, a famous mathematician and cosmographer from Perugia. He took three years to complete the job (1580 to 1583). His signature appears in the long inscription on the Map of Salento. The maps are arranged in topographical order along the gallery, divided by a North-South axis ideally represented by the Apennines. This is explained by the artist himself in a letter of 1580 to the Flemish cartographer Abraham Oertel: "I have been summoned to Rome to devise a description of Italy in a Gallery built by His Holiness. Having divided Italy along the Apennines, I placed on one side of the Gallery the part washed by the Ligurian and Tyrrhenian Seas, and on the other side the part demarcated by the Adriatic Sea and the Alps, dividing it into forty parts by states and prefectures...".

As with other maps from the same period, apart from purely geographical details, these too have numerous inscriptions and decorations illustrating historical events, monuments and characteristics of the various places depicted: for example, the seas are crowded with ships, sea monsters and mythological figures. It is clar from this that Danti aimed to create a work at once geographical and artistic, and for this reason chose to highlight the aesthetic aspects of cartography.

In preparing his cartoons, the Dominican friar undertook meticulous background study, analyzing not only extant drawings and maps but also making on-site visits and examining the work of other cartographers living in the various Italian regions. Views and plans of the main cities have been added to the maps of the regions. some were added at a later period as evinced by the famous map of Rome which shows the towering obelisks commissioned by Sixtus V (1585-1590) and the column in the square of St Mary Major, erected by Paul V (1605-1621). The maps have been restored many times under the pontificates of Sixtus V, Clement VIII (1592-1605), Urban VIII (1623-1644) who commissioned Lucas Holste to supervise the retouching of the paintings, though in some cases this involved a complete remake, Clement XI (1700-1721) and Pius IX (1846-1878), to name but a few.

Gallery of the Candelabra,
left, *view of the Gallery*
right, *Ganymedes and the Eagle*
below, *Ganymedes*

Though this form of decoration had been used previously in other places - such as the Globe Room in Palazzo Vecchio in Florence where Danti himself had painted the then-known parts of the world on the doors of the wardrobes, or the third Vatican Loggia where a cycle of geographical frescoes had been commissioned by Gregory XIII - this is the first example of maps being used to decorate a gallery.

The Gallery of the Candelabra, 80 m long, was commissioned by Pius VI (1775-1799) who ordered Simonetti and Camporese to close an open loggia built by Clement XIII (1758-1769) in 1761. The gallery, divided into six areas by arches resting on columns, is so called for the marble candelabra it contains, a numerous series of Roman manufacture, mostly from excavations at St Constance and St Agnes on the Via Nomentana, and at Otricoli. They are positioned in the rectangular spaces on either side of each arch.

Resting on the capitals, an entablature runs around the entire perimeter of the gallery except over the windows. The entablature supports the ceiling, six barrel vaults with lunettes and a decoration commissioned by Leo XIII (1878-1903) from Domenico Torti and Ludwig Seitz between 1883 and 1887, depicting episodes from his pontificate.

The gallery holds many sculptures and sarcophagi from the classical age, as well as a series of 2nd-century AD frescoes with *Satyrs and Nymphs* found in Rome in the area of Tor Marancia between 1817 and 1823. Among significant works are the small statues of a *Young Boy playing with a Walnut* of the Hellenistic school, and a *Child strangling a Goose*, a marble copy of a 3rd-century BC bronze original. There are also various sarcophagi from the 2nd and 3rd centuries AD with bas-reliefs depicting *Scenes from the myth of Protesilaos*, episodes from the *Myth of Orestes, Scenes from the Myth of Bacchus*, the *Slaughter of the Niobids*, and finally the *Abduction of King Leucippus' two daughters by the Dioscuri*; statues of the *Ephesian Artemis, Apollo, Atalanta* and small

sculptures of *Nike, Tyche of Antioch* and a *Persian Warrior*. Also worthy of note is the copy of a bronze group by Leochares showing *Ganymede and the Eagle*, made by 2nd-century AD Roman copyists and used to decorate the support of a table.

The Gallery of Paintings (now of Tapestries) was founded in 1790, also by Pius VI who in 1789 had had its ceiling decorated by Bernardino Nocchi, Domenico Del Frate and Antonio Marini with allegories in chiaroscuro honouring the glories of the pontiff. The present arrangement of the gallery - which previously housed a picture collection - is due to Gregory XVI (Bartolomeo Cappellari 1831-1846) who, around 1838, decided to use it to display a series of tapestries. The most important works kept here are the tapestries of the so-called New School, woven by the workshops of Pieter van Aelst in Brussels following drawings by pupils of Raphael, and given to Clement VII (1523-1534) before 1531 to be used in papal consistories. The tapestries of the Old School, made using cartoons by Raphael himself during the reign of Leo X (1513-1521), are now on display in the Vatican Pinacoteca.

These tapestries are hung on the left wall of the gallery and depict the following episodes: the *Adoration of the Shepherds*, the *Adoration of the Magi*, the *Introduction of Jesus to the Temple*, the *Slaughter of the Innocents* (repeated three times), the *Resurrection of Christ, Jesus appearing to Mary Magdalene*, and the *Supper in Emmaus*.

On the opposite wall are tapestries representing *Scenes from the life of Urban VIII*, made between 1663 and 1679 by the Roman manufacturer Barberini, founded in 1627 by one of the pope's nephews, Cardinal Francesco Barberini.

Apart from these works, the gallery also holds two 16th-century tapestries ascribable to the Flemish school and the workshops of Vigevano: the *Conversion of the Centurion Cornelius* and the *Death of Julius Caesar*.

In 1884, when Carlo Ludovico Visconti became director general of the Museum, the gallery was restored and three years later a special school for tapestries was founded, forerunner of the present Restoration Laboratory of Tapestries, which has the task of preserving the various examples kept in the Vatican.

BORGIA APARTMENT

The Borgia Apartment derives its name from the family name of Pope Alexander VI (1492-1503) who lived there during the years of his pontificate. The apartment is located on the first floor of the then Vatican Apostolic Palace, which had been built between the 13th and 15th centuries. It currently houses part of the Collection of Modern Religious Art.

Specifically, the name is used to indicate the so-called "secret rooms", that is Alexander VI's private chambers. Their decoration was the result of an ambitious artistic project devised by the newly-elected pope. He chose Bernardino di Betto, known as Pinturicchio, as the man to interpret his Moresque Hispanic tastes, a legacy of his Valencian origins (his secular name was Rodrigo de Borja y Doms).

Pinturicchio had many assistants, among them Pietro d'Andrea da Volterra, Benedetto Bonfigli and Antonio da Viterbo known as Pastura. The iconography, inspired by humanistic ideas, was conceived by men of letters within the Curia and by the artist himself.

The first room, the so-called Room of the Sibyls, takes its name from the subjects represented in the lunettes. It is located in the Borgia Tower, built by Alexander VI between 1492 and 1494 to defend the palace from any external attack. The Sibyls - an allusion to the pagan world - are twined with Prophets, representing the Christian world. The octagonal panels, decorated with the *Astrological Symbols* of the seven major planets, have been attributed to Pastura.

The Room of the Creed is also in the Borgia Tower. Twelve wall lunettes contain half-length busts of *Prophets and Apostles with scrolls reproducing the words of the Creed*, underlining the connection between the Old and New Testaments. This is again a work by members of the school, probably Pastura or Tiberio d'Assisi.

Next is the Room of the Liberal Arts, the first in a series of rooms in the wing of the palace built by Nicholas V (1447-1455). Most probably it was the pontiff's studio, and it is the place where his body was laid after his death. The seven big lunettes are dedicated to the *Liberal Arts of the Trivium* (literary) *and Quadrivium* (scientific), portrayed as beautiful women on thrones, each identified by an inscription. Astronomy, Grammar, Dialectic, Rhetoric, Geometry, Arithmetic and Music are accompanied by exponents of 15th-century culture symbolising the various disciplines: the man of letters Paolo Cortesi, as Cicero, in Rhetoric, and perhaps Bramante, as Euclid, kneeling before Geometry. Pinturicchio's name is visible on the base of the throne of Rhetoric. Only some of the frescoes

Borgia Apartment, Pinturicchio,
Room of the Sibyls, Jeremiah and Agrippa
pages 100 and 101, *Room of the Saints, Disputation of St Catherine of Alexandria*

PINTURICCHIO'S INVENTIVE GRACE

Bernardino di Betto, born in Perugia around 1454, became famous with the nickname of Pinturicchio (he himself used it as a signature), a reference to his modest stature. His was a refined and graceful taste, much appreciated by his contemporaries, although this good fortune which did not accompany him in the judgement of artistic critics, which was heavily influenced by Giorgio Vasari's views in his *Lives*: "although he produced a lot of works, and was helped by many, yet was his name greater than his works deserved".

The Umbrian painter probably undertook his artistic apprenticeship with Bartolomeo Caporali and not - as Vasari maintains - in the workshop of Pietro Perugino, who was only four years his senior. There is no doubt that the latter had a large hand in the stylistic development of the young Bernardino, if for no other reason, at least for Perugino's powerful ascendancy and for the fact that they worked together in Umbria (*Stories of St Bernardino*, Perugia, National Gallery of Umbria) and Rome (decoration of part of the side walls of the Sistine Chapel). However this is inadequate to justify such a personal artistic style, which also was probably influenced by Verrocchio. Pinturicchio's outstanding decorative sense is perhaps due to an apprenticeship in the art of miniature.

His exquisite rendition of architecture, his characters wrapped in watered drapes effortlessly reflecting the shining beauty of the colours and the gold decorations, his taste for reinterpreting Roman fresco decorations dating back to imperial times, all made him an exponent of a sort of "cold Renaissance", in ideal counterpoise to his Florentine contemporaries and to Perugino himself.

Borgia Apartment, Room of the Sibyls, Baruch and Samia

in the Room are attributed to the Umbrian master. The rest were probably the work of Tiberio d'Assisi and Pastura.

The Room of the Liberal Arts leads to other small areas including the pontiff's bedroom and the treasure chamber. The cubicle contains fragments with pillars and open arches over landscapes, part of the decoration made by Pinturicchio and his assistants.

The Room of the Saints, more obviously typical of Pinturicchio, holds representations of the *Martyrdom of St Sebastian* (in the background are the Coliseum and the Palatine with the church of Sts John and Paul), *Susan and the old Men*, the *Stories of St Barbara*, the *Disputation of St Catherine of Alexandria* at the court of Emperor Maximinus (in the background is the Arch of Constantine), the *Visit of St Anthony Abbot and St Paul the Hermit*, and the *Visitation*. The frescoes contain numerous portraits of historical characters, contemporaries of Pinturicchio. On the vault is the *Myth of Isis, Osiris and the Bull Apis*, a very rare iconographic theme for the Renaissance and precious historical testimony to the rediscovery of Egyptian civilisation at that time. The *Madonna with Child* over the door leading to the next room, the Room of the Mysteries of the Faith, is also by Pinturicchio.

This room takes its name from the cycle in the lunettes representing the *Seven Mysteries of the Faith* (the Mysteries of Christ's life contrasted with the Joyful Mysteries of Mary's life). The paintings portray the *Annunciation, Nativity, Adoration of the Magi, Resurrection,* *Ascension, Pentecost* and *Assumption of the Virgin*. In the scene of the Resurrection, the master's direct intervention is evident in the portrayal of Alexander VI absorbed in prayer. It has been suggested, however, that the overall cycle, which is a weaker execution, is the work of the Lombard painter, Bartolomeo di Giovanni.

This room marks the end of works attributable to Pinturicchio.

The last room, the Room of the Popes, marks the beginning of the reception halls, a kind of *trait d'union* between the private areas of the Borgia Apartment and the public areas of the Room of the Vestments, the Sala Ducale and the Sala Regia. The original ceiling supported by wooden beams collapsed in 1500 in the presence of Pope Alexander VI, who miraculously escaped the disaster that cost the lives of many of those present. The current ceiling dates from the pontificate of Leo X (1513-1521). It is decorated with stuccoes and frescoes by Perin del Vaga and Giovanni da Udine.

This beautiful cycle of paintings is a typical example of late 15th-century figurative art, a vivid adaptation of rigorous humanistic culture to the requirements and tastes of the Spanish pope. Pinturicchio, an expert decorator, created exquisite colourful compositions, embellished with the lavish use of gold still typical of mediaeval art. History, in these wall paintings, seems almost a pretext to depict ornamental Nature, in which the portrayal of many classical buildings reveals the typically Renaissance desire to bring the ancient world back to life.

Borgia Apartment, Room of the Liberal Arts,
Pinturicchio, Geometry
left, *Music*

ROOMS OF RAPHAEL

"His beauty is a beauty of reason and not of the eyes" said the neo-classical painter Anton Raphael Mengs commenting Raphael's art. In contrast to the energetic dynamism of Michelangelo, Raphael, the artist from Urbino, had his own stylistic roots in the legacy of the great "logicians" of the early Renaissance, such as Piero della Francesca and Melozzo da Forlì. His classicism - influenced by the artistic environment of Rome after the discovery of the sculptural group of the Laocoon in 1506 - was a grandiose expression of intellect, a solemn pictorial depiction of the philosophical truths underlying nature, and the exterior appearance of man.

In the Vatican *Stanze* (Rooms), Raphael interpreted ancient thought in the light of Christian-humanistic doctrine. The complex iconography, probably conceived by a scholar of the Roman Curia (among others, the names of Ludovico Ariosto and of Celio Calcagnini have been suggested), sought to re-affirm the central role of the Church. The Vatican *Stanze* were, in fact, the apartments of Pope Julius II (Giuliano della Rovere 1503-1513), who had refused to live in the rooms occupied by his predecessor, the Borgia Pope Alexander VI (1492-1503). There are four rooms, all rectangular and with cross vaults, located on the second floor of the Pontifical Palace directly over the Borgia Apartment. The first three had been part of the residence of Nicholas V (1447-1455), the fourth is larger and dates back to the pontificate of Nicholas III (1277-1280).

The commission to decorate the ceilings had been awarded to a group of artists from various parts of Italy - Perugino and Peruzzi from central Italy, Sodoma, Bramantino and Lotto from the north - and to the German Johannes Ruysch who was an expert in grotesque works. In 1508, Bramante brought Raphael to the Vatican. He was from Bramante's hometown and at the time was working in Florence. Once Raphael started work on the Room of the Segnatura, the pope, having noted his undisputed artistic merit, soon decided to commission the entire decoration to him, and dismissed the other painters. For the twenty-five-year-old Raphael this was his first big official commission.

According to Vasari, the walls of the four rooms had been previously decorated by Piero della Francesca, Bartolomeo della Gatta and Luca Signorelli; however the pontiff ordered their work be erased in order to make way for the frescoes of Raphael, who remained involved in this enterprise from 1508 until 1520, the year of his death. It was completed by his helpers in 1524.

Raphael's Rooms, Room of the Segnatura,
left and above, *School of Athens, details*
pages 108 and 109, *School of Athens*

Raphael began by painting the ceiling of the Room of the Segnatura and then continued by frescoing the walls, which were finished in 1511. The iconography, with its exalted conceptual contents, was probably conceived with an eye to the original use of the room, which housed Julius II's studio and library. Afterwards, Pope Leo X (1513-1521) would listen to music here, and he also used it to keep his collection of musical instruments. Later still, it became the seat of the Court of the *Signatura Gratiae et Iustitiae*.

The frescoes illustrate the ideal order of humanistic culture through the three categories of Truth, Goodness and Beauty. In medallions on the vault are four allegorical figures symbolising four disciplines: *Theology, Philosophy, Law* and *Poetry*. These are reflected in the scenes depicted on the walls below. Truth is shown as revealed truth in the *Disputation on the Blessed Sacrament*, and as natural or rational truth in the *School of Athens*, Goodness is symbolised in the depictions of

Raphael's Rooms, Room of the Segnatura,
view of the Room
above, *detail of the vault*

the *Virtues* and of the *Law* (civil law in *Tribonian giving the Pandects to Justinian*, and canon law in *Gregory IX approves the Decretalia*). Finally, Beauty is expressed through *Poetry* in the *Parnassus*.

The *Disputation on the Blessed Sacrament* is so-called following the incorrect interpretation of Giorgio Vasari. The work really represents the triumph of religion. It consists of two parts. The lower shows the Church militant made up of doctors and theologians, positioned on two convergent diagonals and attendant upon the Sacrament of the Eucharist, the real centre and focal point of the entire scene. The upper portion of the work depicts the Church triumphant: in the middle at the top is God the Father surrounded by angels, in the centre Christ in Majesty between the Virgin and St John and, underneath, the dove symbolizing the Holy Spirit. Surrounding this representation of the Trinity are saints and the just of the Old Testament sitting upon a crown of clouds in the form of a semicircle. Among the characters in the lower part are St Gregory the Great in the likeness of Julius II, Fra Angelico, Girolamo Savonarola, Dante, Bramante, Francesco Maria della Rovere, and many others, almost as if to continue the 15th-century tradition of portraying contemporary figures alongside others from the past.

Opposite the *Disputation*, the *School of Athens* portrays a host of thinkers, philosophers and scientists of antiquity. In the background is an ancient building, probably inspired by Bramante's plans for the new St Peter's.

In the centre Plato, holding the *Timaeus* in his hand, points towards the sky while Aristotle, carrying his *Ethics*, turns the palm of his hand towards the earth. Among the multitude of philosophers is, on the left of the two main characters, Socrates with his characteristic Silenus profile in the act of talking to a group of young men. Zeno is at the bottom on the far left near Epicurus who is crowned by vine leaves and reading a book; Pythagoras is writing in a large volume, and behind him is Averroes wearing a turban. Heraclitus is resting his elbow on a marble block, and Diogenes is lying on the steps. To the right, Euclid is measuring a geometric figure with a compass and behind him are Zoroaster and Ptolemy, respectively holding the heavenly and the earthly spheres. Some of the characters in the painting have the likeness of contemporary figures: Leonardo as Plato, Michelangelo as Heraclitus and Bramante as Euclid, to name just a few.

This work is universally considered to be entirely Raphael's own, as attested by what is probably the artist's signature on Euclid's collar: R.V.S.M. (*Raphaël Urbinas Sua Manu*). The fresco, which had immediate and enormous appeal from the moment it was unveiled, has

Raphael's Rooms, Room of the Segnatura, Parnassus, detail

Raphael's Rooms, Room of the Segnatura,
Disputation on the Blessed Sacrament
left and above,
Disputation on the Blessed Sacrament, details

THE MANNER OF DIVINE RAPHAEL

"… Disciple of beautiful nature and of its great ideas [...] which Plato says is the most perfect original of beautiful things". Thus the 17th-century French theorist André Félibien defined Raphael Sanzio of Urbino.

Inspired by the principle of beauty deriving from scrutiny of ancient objects, Raphael more than other artists devised a form of painting of great clarity, which rose to become the emblem of all 16th-century Italian painting. In his name, and after his early death, a unifying artistic language was born. Vasari himself, using the expression "modern manner", sought to exalt the achievements of Raphael, Michelangelo and Leonardo, whose art was even higher than the nature whence those three masters drew their inspiration. For a better understanding of this, it is undoubtedly useful to read Vasari's *Lives* where the author clarifies the various meanings of the term "manner". He starts by describing manner as a synonym of "style" or the "a way of expression" of an artist; a way that is absorbed and reproduced by the pupils of his school. A century earlier, Cennini had anticipated this interpretation recognising in "manner" the typical features of an age or of a geographic area. In the Proem of the *Third Age*, Vasari argues that manner is one of the fundamental factors of progress - used to overcome and, at the same time, to imitate nature - and that the highest results in this field were achieved by the three main exponents of the Renaissance.

Raphael - more than Leonardo and Michelangelo - was taken as a model of order and harmony; this was something completely new and absolutely unprecedented, and the concept of artistic imitation changed radically: the motif to imitate was no longer sought in nature itself, but in the works of those masters who in nature had deliberately sought their inspiration.

The definition of Mannerism (the term was used for the first time by the Jesuit Luigi Lanzi towards the end of the 18th century) was employed, then, to indicate those artists of the second half of the 16th century who referred back to the great Renaissance masters; but it was applied as a term of condemnation for an art seen only as cold imitation and lacking naturalness. Mannerism was seen merely as filling the artistic-chronological gap between the Renaissance and the Baroque. It lost its negative connotations only at the beginning of the 20th century when that period, previously considered as lacking in authentic inspiration, was reappraised.

Raphael's Rooms, Room of the Segnatura,
Disputation of the Holy Sacrament, detail

Raphael's Rooms, Room of Heliodorus,
view of the Room
above, *Raphael, Mass of Bolsena, detail*

Raphael's Rooms, Room of Heliodorus,
view of the Room
above, *Raphael, Liberation of St Peter, detail*

also been interpreted as representing the seven Liberal Arts: Grammar and Arithmetic (in the statues of Apollo and Minerva), Music (in the group in the foreground on the left), Geometry and Astronomy (in the figures on the right), Rhetoric and Dialectic (in the characters at the top).

The third great work in the Room of the Segnatura is the *Parnassus*, which according to classical myth is the mountain sacred to Apollo and the Muses. In the scene, Apollo is playing the "lira da braccio" surrounded by the nine Muses of the Arts. On the left of the fresco are Ennius, Dante, Homer (as Laocoon), Virgil and Statius. Below them, Alcaeus, Corinna, Petrarch, Anacreon and Sappho. In the group on the right are some Italian men of letters including Tebaldeo, Boccaccio, Tibullo, Ariosto, Properzio, Ovid and Sannazzaro. At the bottom is Horace. This parallelism between classical and modern poets in the *Parnassus* is evidence of the ever-closer relationship to the world of *latinitas*, something that Raphael, in accordance with the views of the humanists, was intent to explore. This work, completed after the *Disputation* and the *School of Athens*, marks the full stylistic maturity of the artist.

Between 1511 and 1514 Raphael and his assistants frescoed the Room of Heliodorus. It derives its name from the subject of one of the wall paintings. The central iconographic theme is that of the Lord's divine protection of His Church, menaced by internal and external enemies. In those years the papacy was trying to defend its temporal power: Julius II, having opposed the expansionist policy of Venice, had to beware his own old ally, France. The situation was deteriorating and amid such uncertainty a show of strength was required. The decision to depict such a subject, and precisely in the place used for papal audiences, aimed to reaffirm pontifical authority.

The episodes depicted on the ceiling and on the walls must be considered as a unit, because they have a common subject matter. The scenes on the vault contain the *Burning Bush*, when God spoke to Moses to free the Israelites from Egyptian slavery; *Jacob's Ladder*, where God appeared in a dream to the patriarch of the Jewish people; the *Apparition of God to Noah*, when God saved Noah from the flood; and the *Sacrifice of Isaac*, during which God rewarded Abraham for his faith. These scenes are related to those depicted on the walls below: the *Expulsion of Heliodorus from the Temple*, the *Deliverance of St Peter*, the *Encounter of Leo the Great with Attila the Hun*, and the *Mass of Bolsena*.

The *Expulsion of Heliodorus* shows the biblical episode of Heliodorus, chancellor of the King of Syria who, having stolen the treasure from

Raphael's Rooms, view of the Room of the Fire in the Borgo

the Temple of Jerusalem, is banished by a divine knight and two youths. The "expulsion" from the Temple alludes to the inviolability of the Church's estates. The artist gives a classical atmosphere to the scene by placing it in a sort of Bramantesque building, decentralising the narrative into two separate parts: on the left is the commissioning pontiff watching the scene, and on the right is the event itself. The intervening space is filled with an architectural perspective. The intellectual meditations typical of Raphael here become dramatically evident in movements and gestures that are normally associated with historical painting.

The *Deliverance of St Peter* is divided into three distinct parts: in the centre, the angel appears to Peter in a dream; on the right, he leads the saint from prison while the guards lie sleeping; on the left, in the light of a torch a soldier wakes the guards who are astonished at the sudden disappearance of their prisoner. This is one of the most captivating nocturnal scenes in the history of art, in which Raphael adopts new stylistic techniques that were destined to have great future impact. The Apostle is depicted as Julius II, a clear reference to the divine intervention in the pontiff's favour against the French invaders. The extraordinarily modern use of light portrays the miraculous event in a kind of snapshot of prodigious splendour; indeed this fresco is one of the most famous in the whole of Raphael's *corpus*.

The *Encounter of Leo the Great and Attila the Hun* is portrayed against the backdrop of Rome wherre the outline of the Coliseum, an aqueduct and a basilica are visible, although the actual historical event took place on the River Mincio near Mantua in 452. Sts Peter and Paul, armed with swords, are in the sky terrorising the barbarians.

The *Mass of Bolsena* depicts a miracle that occurred in Bolsena in 1263 when a Bohemian priest, in doubt about the Presence of Christ in the Eucharist, saw some drops of blood trickling from the Consecrated Host. The episode led to the establishment of the Feast of *Corpus Domini* and the building of the duomo of Orvieto. Raphael chose to divide the surface to be frescoed into two parts: on one side is the miracle taking place before Pope Julius II who, as a spectator and witness to the event, is portrayed on the other side together with his court. The intense effect of light diffusing into the scene helps to absorb the dramatic tension in an elegant composite balance, made even more harmonious by the distinction between the main figures and the characters to the sides and below.

The Room known as the Fire in the Borgo from the subject of one of the scenes, was originally the seat of the highest Pontifical Court, the *Signatura Gratiae*, which met only under the presidency of the pon-

Raphael's Rooms, Room of the Fire in the Borgo, Raphael and pupils,
Battle of Ostia
pages 126 and 127, *Fire in the Borgo*

tiff. Later, though, it became the common dining room of Leo X's apartments, the so-called *tinello segreto*. It was the last to be painted by Raphael, between 1514 and 1517, although it is clear that a considerable portion was done by his helpers. In fact, at that time, Raphael was involved in taking over from Bramante as architect of St Peter's, and had also been appointed as Superintendent of Antiquities in Rome.

The subject matter of the frescoes aims to exalt the conciliatory policies being put into effect by Pope Leo X. To this end, they depict events from the past in which other popes of the name Leo played a leading role.

One of the scenes shows the *Coronation of Charlemagne*, which took place in the Vatican Basilica on Christmas Eve in the year 800 at the hands of Leo III, the act marking the foundation of the Holy Roman Empire. The Carolingian sovereign is portrayed as Francis I of France, and Leo III as Leo X, a reference to the concordat drawn up between the pontiff and Francis I at Bologna in 1515.

The *Oath of Leo III* shows the pope swearing an oath before Charlemagne and the clergy in the basilica of St Peter on the day before the coronation of the sovereign, denying the accusations made against him by the nephews of Hadrian I, while from on high a voice admonishes *Dei non hominum est episcopos iudicare*. This a clear allusion to the 1516 Lateran Council's reaffirmation of the principle contained in Boniface VIII's Bull *Unam Sanctam* according to which the pontiff is accountable for his actions only to God.

The fresco of the *Fire in the Borgo* shows an episode dating from the year 847, described in the *Liber Pontificalis*, when Leo IV, making the sign of the cross, miraculously extinguished a fire which had broken out in the area of the Borgo near St Peter's in Rome. The pontiff may be seen in the background, at the Loggia of Blessings of the old basilica of Constantine. The foreground scene is more dramatic as the terrified multitudes pour out from houses and streets trying to escape the flames. The group on the left recalls Aeneas escaping

from Troy and epitomises the charity of a man who saves his family. The woman saving her child is an emblem of maternal love, while the nudity of the figure hanging from the wall adds a heroic dimension to the depiction of a man in a moment of terror. The group on the right, fetching buckets to extinguish the fire, convey agitation and anxiety, while the group of women in the centre, protecting their children and invoking the pontiff's help, represent smothers' desperation. Leo IV's act in saving his people is thus linked to the peace mission being carried out by Leo X in those years.

The *Liber Pontificalis* is also the source that inspired the last fresco in the room, the *Battle of Ostia*, which celebrates the victory of Leo IV over the Saracens on the coast near Rome in the year 849. The political programme of Leo X, whose physical features may be seen in the face of the 9th-century pontiff, included a crusade against the Turks and this fresco is a clear allusion to that event.

The ceiling fresco by Perugino, with allegorical figures inside medallions, was left untouched by the master from Urbino.

The last of the *Stanze*, in chronological order of completion, is the Room of Constantine, the so-called *caenaculum amplior*, a room designed for receptions, official ceremonies and solemn banquets. The decorations were completed between 1520 and 1524 by Raphael's pupils, especially by Giulio Romano and Giovan Francesco Penni, on the basis of drawings left by the master prior to his premature death on 6th April 1520.

The fresco cycle, commissioned by Leo X but completed during the pontificate of Clement VII (1523-1534), celebrates the Church by depicting the main events from the story of Constantine who, with the Edict of Milan in 313 AD, became the first Roman emperor to grant freedom of worship to Christians. The first episode is the *Vision of the Cross*: as Constantine talks to his soldiers before the battle against Maxentius, the Cross appears in the sky accompanied by the Greek words: "under this sign you will triumph". In the wake of this event, Constantine defeated his rival and began supporting the Church. The next scene, the *Battle of Ponte Milvio*, celebrates his

Raphael's Rooms, Room of the Fire in the Borgo, Perugino, detail of ceiling, papal coat-of-arms
right, *detail of ceiling*

victory over Maxentius, while the third, the *Baptism of Constantine*, portrays the emperor as he receives the sacrament in the Baptistery of St John Lateran; the book before the celebrant bears the words *Hodie salus Urbi et Imperio facta est*. In the last panel, the *Donation of Rome*, the emperor is shown inside the Vatican Basilica granting Pope Sylvester temporal power over the city of Rome and the West. The reference here is to the legendary tale contained in the famous *Donatio Costantini*, a document written in the early Middle Ages but considered in later centuries to be an original dating back to Constantine. In the 15th century, Lorenzo Valla proved it to be a forgery by illustrating how the Latin used in the text of the *Donatio* was not from late antiquity. The decision to depict such themes reveals a desire to underline the hegemonic role of the Church by analysing a significant moment in her history: the period in which she was becoming an institution and her complete triumph over paganism. The present ceiling of the room is the work of Tommaso Laureti and Antonio Scalvati in 1585.

The Vatican *Stanze* are one of Raphael's finest masterpieces. The custom of calling them by the name of the artist rather than by the names of the commissioning popes came into use six months after the death of the master and is a testament to the esteem in which his art was held. These rooms gave Raphael the opportunity to treat various subjects by using different techniques according to the message he wished to communicate. First are the characters in the Room of the Segnatura who move in mental rather than in real space and, raised to the rank of bearers of truth, express the wisdom of the ancient world and that of Christian spirituality. Later, the artist abandoned doctrinal themes and concentrated on history and panegyric, achieving levels of great intensity as in the scene of the *Fire in the Borgo*. Thus the *Stanze* are an expression of universal art founded on the idea of balance and on the ideal of classical beauty that embraces all forms of thought: an art that dominated ancient as well modern times.

Raphael's Rooms, view of the Room of Constantine

LOGGIAS OF RAPHAEL

The Vatican Loggias were built during the pontificates of Julius II (1503-1513) and Leo X (1513-1521). They consist of three floors of porticos respectively in the Doric, Ionic and Corinthian orders (in keeping with the model of famous Roman monuments such as the Coliseum and the Theatre of Marcellus), and were built with the aim of creating a majestic façade for the eastern end of the old palace of Nicholas III (1277-1280). The design of the imposing frontage is Bramante's, although the idea of three superimposed loggias came to him from the solutions adopted in the corresponding wall of the mediaeval edifice which, according to scholars, already had two orders of arched galleries over a portico. Bramante envisioned a new structure, following the classical models then predominant, and he worked on it until his death in 1514, completing the first floor. The task of completing the project was entrusted to Raphael who made some modifications to the original plans. For example, for the bays of the second order - the only one to be known by the name of Loggia of Raphael - he built "pavilion" vaults rather than the domes envisaged by Bramante, in order to increase the surface area for frescoes.

As regards the decoration, the Doric and Corinthian levels are the work of a pupil of Raphael, Giovanni da Udine, who did the first round of work on his own and was helped by other artists for the second. The design for the pictorial cycle of the Ionic order is entirely Raphael's. He supervised the work and provided the preparatory drawings However, critics do not agree as to its actual execution, which is attributed to various artists of his workshop: Giulio Romano, Giovan Francesco Penni, Giovanni da Udine, Tommaso Vincidor, Pellegrino da Modena, Perin del Vaga, Vincenzo Tamagni, Polidoro da Caravaggio, Raffaellino del Colle, Guillaume de Marcillat and Pedro Machuca.

The Loggia of Raphael is made up of thirteen small bays with vaulted ceilings. All the vaults follow the same pattern: four panels depicting biblical episodes set to form the arms of a cross inscribed within a square with, at its centre, a panel with a white stucco angel carrying, alternatively, the papal ring with three plumes (red, green and white) symbolising the Theological Virtues, or a yoke with the words *Jugum enim meum suave est, et onus meum leve,* a reference to the governmental skills of Leo X. Only the centre panel of the middle vault has the Medici coat-of-arms of the pontiff who commissioned the work. These frescoes partly follow those on the ceiling of the Sistine Chapel, covering the same subject matter and depicting, in the first twelve vaults, *Stories from the Old Testament,* and in the thirteenth, *Episodes from the New Testament.* The main difference to Michelangelo's cycle of frescoes is the explicit reference to antiquity underlying the entire decoration of the loggia, the origins of which are to be sought in the antiquarian taste of the pontiff and in the archaeological interests that Raphael had been developing ever since his arrival in Rome. Surrounding the scenes in their classic-style frames, the intervening spaces are filled with decorations of various types: coffers adorned with angels, illusionistic colonnades or fake painted architectural forms reaching up to skies full of birds, or tapestries decorated with grotesques. The background to the frescoes in the central vault is unique, made up of candelabra and a white and golden stucco portico in which nymphs dance. The whole area is covered in a variety of stuccoes with mythological themes, grotesques and festoons with flowers, fruit and vegetal motifs.

The cycle of biblical stories contained in the vaults of the loggia and in monochrome works at the bottom of each bay, is divided as follows:

The first vault contains Stories from Genesis: *God separates light from darkness, God separates land from water, God creates the sun and the moon, God creates the animals*; at the base, *God blesses the seventh day.*

The second vault contains the Stories of Adam and Eve: the *Creation of*

Loggias of Raphael, Second Loggia, Raphael and pupils,
seventh vault, Stories of Joseph,
detail of Joseph telling his dreams to his brethren
left, *view of the Loggia*

Eve, *Original Sin, Expulsion from Paradise, Adam and Eve labouring*; below are *Cain and Abel*.

The third vault is dedicated to the Stories of Noah: *Building of the Ark*, the *Flood, Leaving the Ark, Sacrifice of Noah*; at the base, *God shows the rainbow to Noah*.

In the fourth vault are the Stories of Abraham and Lot: the biblical episode of the *Meeting of Abraham with Melchizedek, God's Covenant with Abraham, Visitation of the angels, Fire and Lot's escape from Sodom*; below, *Sacrifice of Isaac*.

The fifth vault illustrates the Stories of Isaac: *God appears to Isaac and forbids him to go to Egypt, Abimelech spies upon Isaac and Rebekah, Isaac blesses Jacob, Isaac blesses Esau*; at the bottom, *Isaac and Esau*.

The sixth vault is adorned with the Stories of Jacob: *Jacob's Dream, Meeting with Rachel at the well, Pact with Laban, Return to Canaan*; at the base, *Jacob fights with the angel*.

The seventh vault presents the Stories of Joseph: *Joseph telling his Dreams to his brothers, Joseph is sold by his brothers, Temptation of Potiphar's wife, Interpreting Pharaoh's dreams*; below, *Joseph is recognised by his brothers*.

The eighth vault has the Stories of Moses: *Finding of Moses in the Nile, Burning Bush, Crossing of the Red Sea, Prodigy of the water springing from the rock*; below is the *Miracle of the manna*.

The Stories of Moses continue in the ninth vault: *Moses receives the Tables of the Law, Worship of the golden calf, Pillar of Fire, Moses shows the Tables of Law to the Hebrews*; below is a scene interpreted either as the *Death of Aaron's children* or *the punishment of the people of Korah*.

The tenth vault depicts the Stories of Joshua: *The Ark crossing the Jordan, Fall of Jericho, Joshua makes the sun and the moon stand still, Dividing the Promised Land*; below, *Joshua speaking to the Hebrews*.

The eleventh vault shows the Stories of David: *Anointment of David, David and Goliath, David's sin, the Triumph of David over the Ammonites*; at

the bottom, *Bathsheba intercedes with David in favour of Solomon.*
The twelfth vault illustrates the Stories of Salomon: *Anointing, Judgement of Solomon, Building of the Temple, Meeting the Queen of Sheba*; below, *Scenes from the life of Solomon.*
The thirteenth vault contains the Stories of Christ: *Adoration of the Shepherds, Adoration of the Magi, Baptism of Jesus, Last Supper*; at the base, *Resurrection.*
The loggias exercised an artistic influence that lasted for more than three centuries, until the neo-classical age. They provided a source of inspiration to countless artists interested in the decorative arts and the reclamation of antiquity. Raphael and his workshop showed a profound knowledge of the classic world, one that reached beyond the mere citation of ancient models to touch upon a direct understanding of the formal ideal underlying Roman ornamental design. These artists worked in what may be described as a "choral" dimension - in

which it is difficult to isolate individual personalities as they painted alongside one another giving life to what is almost a common language - creating a private area for the pontiff in which to pursue his intellectual digressions; a place where the ancient could relive through the architecture, decoration and statues adorning the gallery: a sort of private museum.

Loggias of Raphael, Second Loggia, Raphael and his pupils,
view of the eighth vault
left, *view of the seventh vault*

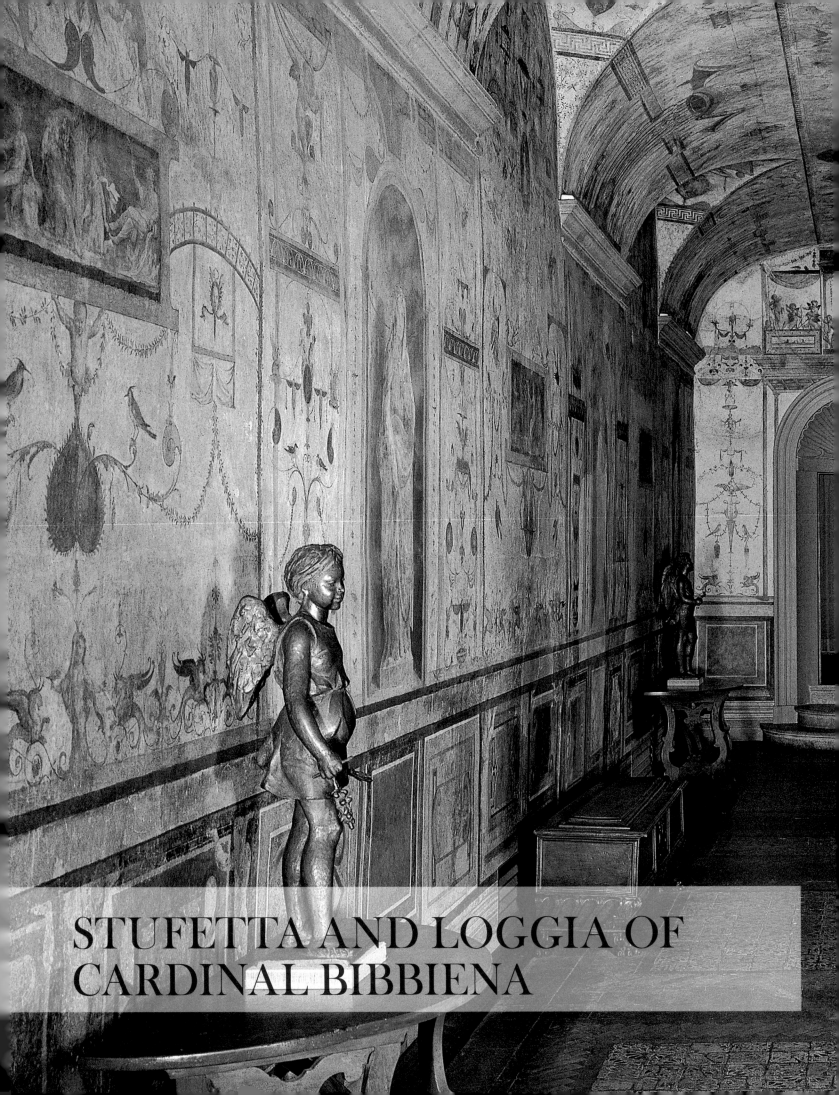

STUFETTA AND LOGGIA OF CARDINAL BIBBIENA

On the third floor of the Vatican Palace, Leo X (1513-1521) had an apartment built for his private secretary, Bernardo Dovizi, known as Bibbiena, cardinal of Santa Maria in Portico. All that now remains of the apartment are a small loggia and the little *stufetta*.

The *stufetta* was a heated bathroom, a sort of small Roman *calidarium* in which heat was generated by hot air circulating through a space within the walls. It was frescoed in 1516 by Raphael's workshop, with the master himself making a vital contribution, at least to the general scheme of the decoration. The paintings on the walls are on two levels: on the lower are small boards on a black background with *Cherubs on chariots*, on the upper are panels with the *Myth of Venus*. On the cross vault over the small quadrangular space are ornamental motifs and mythological scenes, alluding to the power of love. The lunettes have grotesque decorations on a red background.

Immediately afterwards the artists began to fresco the *Loggetta*, or small loggia. This is a rectangular area, about 16 m long, almost completely covered with frescoed grotesques on a white background, as is the case in some places of Nero's *Domus Aurea*. Covering the area is a lowered and barrel-vaulted ceiling with lunettes, upon which is painted a pergola crowded with small images of animals and monsters. The pergola is "supported" by slim colonnades painted on the walls and covered by small figures. On the interior walls of the loggia are panels on a black background that depict the *Myth of Apollo and Marsyas*, while female figures (interpreted as the *Four Seasons*) stand in the guise of statues in *trompe-l'oeil* niches. The images almost absorbed by the wall decoration, meld into the covering of grotesques without interrupting it.

In the cardinal's apartment, Raphael and his school created a world inhabited by small forms, completely disassociated from the plastic images with which the group of artists had previously been engaged, and in part was still working on in the Vatican *Stanze*.

What emerges is the atmosphere of Roman "compendium" painting, aroused by Raphael's interest in the frescoes of the *Domus Aurea*; an atmosphere also present in the decorations of the second floor of the Vatican Loggias.

SISTINE CHAPEL

The Sistine Chapel, built by Sixtus IV (Francesco della Rovere 1471-1484) and dedicated to the Assumption, stands on the place once occupied by the "great chapel", a mediaeval structure in which popes celebrated solemn liturgies, greeted ambassadors and held meetings of the pontifical court. Architectural analyses undertaken during recent restorations have revealed how the present building incorporates part of the walls of the previous one, which must also have been an imposing edifice. The current building has the same rectangular plan as the old, and covers the same dimensions: 40 metres long and 13.5 metres wide.

For the first six years of his pontificate, Sixtus IV used the mediaeval building, but in 1477 decided to have it completely restored. It is still not clear, even today, whether the work was carried out by Giovannino de' Dolci or Baccio Pontelli. De' Dolci received payment for building the chapel but it is perhaps more plausible to consider him as a sort of "foreman" rather than as the architect. Pontelli, a skilled architect and pupil of Francesco di Giorgio Martini, was at the court of Federico da Montefeltro in Urbino at that time and therefore, in order to give him an active role in the project, we must assume he sent his plans to Rome. The solution is perhaps offered by Vasari who says that the commissioned architect was Pontelli, but the work was carried out by Giovannino de' Dolci.

Below the chapel structure are two more floors, a basement level and a mezzanine level. This area once housed the offices of the *Magistri Caeremoniarum*, the masters of ceremonies. Today it houses the Collection of Modern Religious Art.

The chapel is a vast hall divided into two parts by a marble screen, one for the clergy and one for the faithful. The screen was originally attached to the lateral *cantoria*, but was moved back to its current position in the 16th century in order to increase the area reserved for religious. Screen and *cantoria* are a pair, clearly made while construction work was still in progress. Both are decorated with fine reliefs, perhaps the work of Mino da Fiesole, Giovanni Dalmata and Andrea Bregno, though not all scholars agree on this attribution. The floor is in the Cosmati style and the chapel is illuminated by twelve arched windows. Building work was probably finished in late 1480, but certainly before the end of 1481 when the pontiff ordered Giovannino de' Dolci to assemble a group of

distinguished painters from the Umbrian and Florentine schools to decorate the walls. They were Perugino, Botticelli, Ghirlandaio and Cosimo Rosselli, with their respective workshops. The four artists signed the contract on 27th October 1481 so establishing a great shared enterprise, which started *a capite altaris*, i.e. from the wall over the altar. None of the group acted as co-ordinator of the entire cycle, and judging by the autonomy each showed in his work it would seem they worked independently, though respecting some common guidelines and planning the overall structure of the paintings together. Countless strategies were used to give uniformity to the cycle: the horizon line, which is at the same height in all the paintings, or the similar dimensions and proportions of the characters. The level of co-operation was such that at times the masters shared their assistants and helped one another.

Later, other skilled artists, among them Luca Signorelli and Biagio d'Antonio Tucci, joined the original group to help complete the cycle, which was probably finished by spring 1482. On 9th August 1483, the anniversary of the election of Pope Sixtus IV, the first Mass was celebrated in the chapel, which was solemnly consecrated on 15th August.

Sistine Chapel,
altar
left, *view of the Chapel*
pages 140 and 141, *Michelangelo, view of the Ceiling*

The theme of the frescoes focuses on the correspondence between the *Life of Moses*, taken from the Old Testament and depicted on the left wall, and the *Life of Christ* from the New Testament, on the right wall. Each pairing of panels, made up of an episode from the Old Testament and one from the Life of Christ, has Latin *tituli* beginning, apart from one pair, with the same word. The fresco cycle has lost its beginning and end: the first two scenes with the *Finding of Moses* and the *Nativity of Christ*, located behind the altar, were destroyed in 1534 when Clement VII (1523-1534) commissioned Michelangelo to paint the *Last Judgement*; and the *Disputation over the body of Moses* and the *Resurrection of Christ*, originally on the wall by the entrance door, were lost in 1522 when the architrave collapsed.

These latter two episodes were over-painted during the pontificate of Pius IV (1559-1565) - respectively by Matteo da Lecce and Hendrick van den Broeck - and for this reason cannot be considered an integral part of the Sistine cycle, apart from their themes which are the same as the originals. Also dating from the 15th century are the fake drapes at the base of the walls below the biblical scenes, and the twenty-eight surviving images of the first *Pontiffs* of the Church, in full-length portraits within painted niches between the clerestory windows. The original star-studded sky by Pier Matteo d'Amelia on the ceiling was lost with Michelangelo's interventions, as was Perugino's fresco of the *Assumption of the Virgin*, the altarpiece of the chapel.

Left Wall:

In keeping with mediaeval tradition, the fresco of the *Journey of Moses in Egypt*, attributed to Perugino and his assistants, condenses the biblical episode by bringing various events together into one scene. In the background Moses, immediately recognisable by his green and yellow robe, bids farewell to his father-in-law Jethro as the Jews begin their journey to Egypt. In the centre foreground Moses meets the angel who tells him that he may go no further unless his wife Zipporah circumcises their second-born. The scene of the child being circumcised is on the right. Almost half the fresco is occupied by groups of figures while, by contrast, the upper part contains a peaceful landscape with light naturalistic details and a mysterious rural dance the significance of which is unclear.

The next panel, representing *Events in the life of Moses*, is by Sandro Botticelli and his workshop. The narrative sequence is from right to left: Moses slaying the Egyptian who mistreated a Hebrew (pre-

Sistine Chapel, left wall, Perugino and helpers, Journey of Moses in Egypt

sumably a reference to Christ overcoming the devil depicted on the facing wall); a woman helping a wounded Hebrew; Moses going to the village of Madian; his struggle with the shepherds who importuned the daughters of Jethro and prevented them from watering their flock at the well. In the upper left, Moses grazes the flock and removes his sandals because God tells him he is on holy ground; Moses kneels before the Burning Bush where he is ordered to free the Hebrews from slavery; and finally, the exodus of the Hebrews from Egypt. The artist was thus able to bring together seven episodes, using an elegant sinusoidal movement to link the narrative sequence.

The fresco of the *Crossing of the Red Sea* is attributed to Biagio d'Antonio Tucci and his helpers. The composition is dominated by the Hebrews who have just crossed the Red Sea and by pharaoh's army engulfed under the waters. On the right, the Elders of Egypt are in a council and in the background the rainbow symbolises the alliance between God and the Hebrews. The scene is somewhat rigid but is nonetheless held together by a certain formalism expressed through an energetic use of drawing that almost gives it the appearance of inventive fantasy.

In the panel of the *Handing over of the Tables of the Law*, the work of Cosimo Rosselli and his collaborators, the narrative sequence follows an original cross pattern. At the centre, the Hebrews are gathered around Moses' brother Aaron, in the act of adoring the golden calf. Above, on Mount Sinai, Moses, depicted as an old man, receives the Tables of the Law, but returning to his people he is enraged by what he sees and breaks them in fury. Later, having again received the Tables from God, he hands them over to the Hebrews who, in the meantime, have been forgiven. In the background on the right is the punishment of the idolaters.

In the *Punishment of Korah, Dathan and Abiram*, Botticelli and his workshop brought together three events. On the right, the youths Caleb and Joshua, who had encouraged the Hebrews to conquer the Promised Land, find themselves along with Moses in the midst of a revolt, the crowd threatening them with stones. In the centre, Moses and Aaron intervene during a revolt that broke out when two youths made illicit sacrifices. It is significant that the Arch of Constantine should be depicted above this scene, celebrating the victory of the emperor over Maxentius and so symbolising the triumph of Christianity over paganism. Over the arch, in place of the original Roman epigraph, are emblematic words taken from the *Epistle to the Hebrews* to the effect that priesthood arises

Sistine Chapel, left wall, Sandro Botticelli and workshop, Events in the Life of Moses

146

*Sistine Chapel, left wall, Biagio
d'Antonio Tucci, Crossing of the Red Sea*
left and above,
Crossing of the Red Sea, detail

149

Sistine Chapel, left wall,
Cosimo Rosselli and assistants,
Handing over of the Tables of Law
left and above,
Handing over of the Tables of Law, detail

NEMO·SIBI·ASSVMM
AT·HONORE·M·NISI·
VOCATVS·ADEO·
TANQVAM·ARON·

Sistine Chapel, left wall, Sandro Botticelli and workshop, Punishment of Korah, Dathan and Abiram
left and above, *Punishment of Korah, Dathan and Abiram, detail*

153

Sistine Chapel, left wall, Bartolomeo
della Gatta, Luca Signorelli, Sandro
Botticelli and unknown Umbrian painter,
Legacy and Death of Moses
left and above,
Legacy and Death of Moses, detail

155

from a divine vocation: NO SIBI ASSVMM / AT HONOREM NISI / VOCATVS A DEO / TANQVAM ARON. To the left is depicted the biblical episode of the rebellion of the people of Korah against Moses and Aaron and the subsequent punishment of the rebels by God, who caused the ground to open under their feet. This scene by Botticelli - symbolically linked to the *Delivery of the Keys* by Perugino on the opposite wall - appears to be sustained by figures that maintain some degree of Gothic refinement, and by a typically Renaissance taste for spectacle. The groups of characters seem to light across the surface of the fresco, as if they were dancing rather than fighting. Botticelli wraps the images in a play of curves, adorning them with sharp, bright colours. The figures seem crystallised in a time impossibly remote yet conserved for the present. The last episode on this wall is the *Legacy and Death of Moses* by Luca Signorelli, Bartolomeo della Gatta, Sandro Botticelli and an unknown Umbrian painter. Five events are depicted: on the left, Moses gives his rod to Joshua declaring him as his successor; on the right, the Hebrews listen to the words of Moses who is seated on the Ark of the Covenant; in the background, an angel on Mount Nebo shows the Promised Land to the Lawgiver who then descends with Joshua; also in the background, on the left, is the great patriarch's death. The scene is very rich in detail and presents a clear division between the lower part, crowded with figures, and the upper, which is dominated by nature and a landscape in long perspective.

Right Wall:

The episode of the *Baptism of Christ* is by Perugino and his workshop. The event that gives the work its name is in the foreground: Jesus receives baptism from John, while God the Father watches from on high surrounded by angels, and the Holy Spirit in the form of a Dove descends upon the Messiah. In the background on the right, Christ delivers a sermon while, on the left, John the Baptist does likewise. Another scene shows John as he approaches the River Jordan. The landscape behind the main scene includes some Roman buildings, including the old basilica of St Peter, the Arch of Septimius Severus and the Coliseum.

The next panel, the *Temptations of Christ*, is by Botticelli and his assistants. Satan's temptations of Christ are depicted in the background. On the left, in a wood that stands in for the desert mentioned in the Gospels, the devil disguised as a monk shows stones to Christ, weak from His long fast, and tells Him to turn them into

Sistine Chapel, right wall, Perugino and workshop, Baptism of Christ

bread. In the centre, Satan invites Christ to throw Himself from the Temple of Jerusalem and be saved by the angels (it is interesting to note that the building is in fact the hospital of the Holy Spirit built near the Vatican by Sixtus IV). Finally, on the right, after Satan has tried to offer Christ the kingdoms of the world from a precipice, he is turned away, while three angels prepare a table for the Redeemer. In the middle left, the angels are shown with Jesus, while at the centre of the work is a crowded scene around an altar.

The *Calling of the first Apostles* is by Ghirlandaio and his helpers. Vasari calls it "the episode when Christ summoned Peter and Andrew from their nets". On the left in the middle distance, Christ is shown talking to the Apostles, who then appear in the foreground kneeling before the Redeemer. On the right, Jesus, now accompanied by Peter and Andrew, calls James and John who will also join them to make up the first small group of followers. The central figure of Christ is the pivot towards which all the lines of the painting seem to converge: the diagonal slopes of the mountains in the background and the flight path of the birds. Ghirlandaio made almost all the figures in the right-hand group portraits of real people, especially luminaries of the Florentine colony in Rome. The colours of the fresco are bright and lively. Ghirlandaio seems to be expressing the idea that the Florentine bourgeois mercantile class, to which he himself belonged, possessed the leisure and wealth to bring ancient times, such as the biblical episode, back to life while maintaining all their solemnity.

The fresco of the *Sermon on the Mount* is attributed to Cosimo Rosselli and his workshop. In the background Christ and the Apostles approach the place whence he will deliver the Beatitudes. In the foreground, Christ on the mount speaks to the crowd gathered before Him, while on the right is the scene of Jesus' curing of the leper after His descent from the mount. The limpid rendition of the landscape as the sun is about to set makes this work a real gem of aesthetic refinement.

The *Consignment of the Keys*, by Perugino, and Luca Signorelli and his workshop, is without doubt the most famous fresco of the entire cycle. Various episodes are shown against a broad, polychrome, paved marble floor. The main scene, which gives its name to the panel, is in the centre foreground and represents Christ giving "the keys of the Kingdom of Heaven" to St Peter kneeling before Him (Mt. 16,19). Behind, on the left, is the payment of the tribute, and on the right the attempted stoning of Christ. In the back-

Sistine Chapel, right wall, Sandro Botticelli and assistants, Temptations of Christ

Sistine Chapel, right wall,
Ghirlandaio and collaborators,
Calling of the first Apostles
left and above,
Calling of the first Apostles, detail

161

ground is an octagonal building with a typically Renaissance dome (probably representing the Temple of Jerusalem) and, to the sides, two depictions of the Arch of Constantine in Rome. The severity of the composition - a sublime allegory on the origins of Church power and the continuity between past and present - is not just the declaration of a great Renaissance master, but a testimony of a whole artistic period which had reached perfect maturity through a complete understanding of perspective.

The scene at the end of the wall, by Cosimo Rosselli and Biagio d'Antonio Tucci and his workshop, is the *Last Supper*. It is the only scene of the whole cycle to be set indoors: Christ and the Apostles are shown at a semi-octagonal table. Judas alone is depicted from behind, facing Christ and with a little demon on his shoulder. In the background beyond the pillars are three events due to take place in the immediate future: the episode of the Garden of the Gethsemane, Judas kissing Christ, and the crucifixion. The close correlation of ceiling, table and floor, restricts the scene within artificially perfect architectural confines, far from the spontaneous naturalism of the other panels of the cycle.

Sistine Chapel, right wall,
Perugino, Luca Signorelli and workshop, Consignment of the Keys
pages 162 and 163, *Cosimo Rosselli and workshop, Sermon on the Mount*

Sistine Chapel, right wall,
Cosimo Rosselli, Biagio d'Antonio Tucci
and workshop, Last Supper
left and above,
Last Supper, detail

MICHELANGELO: THE ORIGINS OF A GENIUS

The highest expression of western art, the main artist of the Italian Renaissance, Michelangelo Buonarroti served his apprenticeship at the workshop of Ghirlandaio, though he soon left, attracted by the Medici collections of ancient art, and completed his formation in the classical environment of the court of Lorenzo the Magnificent.

Of all the arts, from the very beginning his preference was for sculpture. Through this medium he studied the movements of the figure in space with a sensitivity to form and volume unequalled in the history of art. Yet he was also able to bring the same qualities to painting and architecture, and it is precisely in this plastic energy that the power of his creative genius lies. Michelangelo was a master of the movement that underlies the tension and momentum of gesture.

The artist was also a poet and wrote in a madrigal:

"Sì come per levar, Donna, si pone / in pietra alpestre e dura / una viva figura, / che là più cresce, u' più la pietra scema, / tal alcun'opre buone, / per l'alma, che pur trema, / cela il soverchio della propria carne / con l'inculta sua cruda e dura scorza".

The pure perfection of the soul resides in the *soverchio*, the "surplus" of the flesh. This is the fundamental truth of his own personal creed. The same Christian principle of the soul that survives the body is given concrete form in a hyperbole which likens the creative gesture of the artist to the act of divine creation.

The rules of Michelangelo's art correspond to an inner reality. They derive from a creative seed within his own mind. The way to make sculptures is to "take off" - in contrast to painting which involves "putting on" - and this means taking away (and hence destroying) matter and freeing the idea. His art is a personal struggle that aims to attain his own interior model.

Sistine Chapel, Ceiling, Michelangelo, Creation of Adam, detail

In 1508, Sixtus IV's nephew Giuliano della Rovere, as Pope Julius II (1503-1513), decided to give a new look to the chapel. To this end, he called on the sublime genius of Michelangelo to devise a new decoration for the vault. Following the rejection of an overly simple original plan based on the depiction of the apostles in the corbels and geometric figures in the central part of the vault, Michelangelo proposed a richer and much more complex design. He took account of the iconography of the 15th-century frescoes, which focused on the story of salvation from Moses to Christ and included the first thirty-two pontiffs of the Church. While fully respecting these themes, the artist decided to add and integrate episodes from *Genesis*.

Over the real vault, Michelangelo painted a monumental architectural structure (made up of five transverse arches) majestically framing the various scenes. Along the centre are episodes from *Genesis*, with pairs of *Ignudi* (nudes) holding figurative medallions. In the middle order, alternating figures of *Prophets* and *Sibyls* are seated on thrones flanked by small pillars. The *Forerunners of Christ* are represented in the lunettes at the top of the walls and in the webs linking them to the ceiling. The four spandrels contain episodes from

the salvation of the people of Israel.

It is remarkable that the Story of Man should have been painted on the ceiling, which is normally the allegory of heaven. Perhaps it seemed the only appropriate place to depict the grandeur of God and His creation. Humanity as represented by the master seems animated by the desire to free itself metaphorically from the very paint of which it is made, and appears to the observer as charged with plastic and tormented dramatic energy.

The faces and gestures of the figures reveal the inner feelings of their soul, yet their nakedness in no way seeks to defy convention. The bodies are those of Michelangelo's sculptures. The artist considered himself essentially as a sculptor - in fact this was his first important painting commission - something borne out in a letter he wrote to his father in January 1509: "my job is not going ahead as I feel it should. That is the difficulty of this job, and all the more so because it is not my profession". These words recall the moments of difficulty Michelangelo must inevitably have faced, especially, we should recall, because he took on such a huge task almost without any help, facing a daily struggle between artistic genius and the physical limits of a man.

Work began in 1508, halted for about a year, and was finally completed between 1510 and 1511. The chapel was inaugurated on 1st November 1512 in the presence of Julius II.

Sistine Chapel, Ceiling,
left and above, *Michelangelo, Ignudi*

Sistine Chapel, Ceiling,
Michelangelo, Creation of Celestial Bodies and Plants
above, *Creation of Celestial Bodies and Plants, detail*

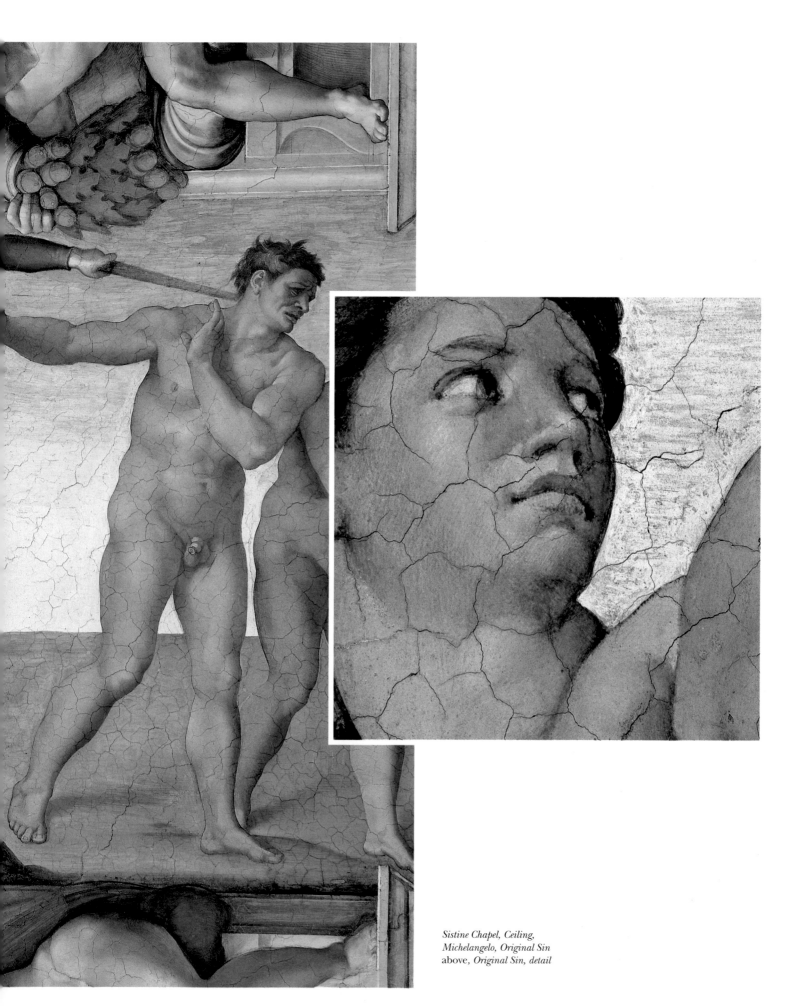

Sistine Chapel, Ceiling,
Michelangelo, Original Sin
above, *Original Sin, detail*

175

The Ceiling:

Biblical stories from the *Book of Genesis* are depicted in nine panels: three dedicated to the creation of the world, three to the story of Adam and Eve, and three to the life of Noah.

The first panel nearest the altar wall shows the *Separation of Light from Darkness*, a reference to the first day of Creation. God the Father is depicted with a bold use of foreshortening, wrapped in pink robes as, with a movement of His hands, He pushes away the darkness and gives origin to the light.

The second panel is the *Creation of Celestial Bodies and Plants*. According to some scholars the double presence of the Almighty - painted from behind while creating vegetaton and from the front, flanked by puttos, while creating the sun and the moon with a double gesture of His hands - is a reference to the fact that these events took place on two days, the third and fourth days of the Bible story. The perfectly rounded perspective of the dual figure is rendered with an admirable use of foreshortening.

God's swirling and imperious movements also predominate in the third panel of the Creation. The Almighty is wrapped in His usual pink robe, this time swollen by winds whence puttos emerge. He is leaning towards the surface of the earth as He effects the *Separation of Land and Sea*, an event that took place on the third day of Creation.

The fourth episode is the famous *Creation of Adam*, an extraordinary and moving representation of the precise instant in which God caused life to be born. The Eternal Father, surrounded by flying angels and wrapped in the same robes as before, is shown as He reaches out to the young man to infuse him with vital energy, while Adam, lying on a rock, stretches out his own hand towards Him.

The next panel along is the famous *Creation of Eve* in which the Almighty gives life to woman and invites her to abandon sleeping Adam from whose rib He generated her. The young man remains lying the while beside a tree trunk. Eve's body leans towards God, who created her in a gesture of love, and her inclined figure and joined hands seem to express her gratitude.

With the *Original Sin* the depiction of the biblical stories begins to become more intricate. The scene is divided into two parts: on the left, Adam and Eve are tempted by the devil in the likeness of an anthropomorphic snake; on the right, they are banished from Eden by an angel brandishing a sword, their bodies irredeemably aged as their sin is also reflected in their outward appearance. The tree marks both the dividing line between the two scenes and

Sistine Chapel, Ceiling, Michelangelo, The Flood

the centre of the composition where it symbolizes the centrality of sin in human history. At the top of the tree is the figure of the snake tempting the first parents and, by contrast, the angel who forcefully drives them away and leaves them to the fate they have chosen.

The seventh scene, the *Sacrifice of Noah*, shows the patriarch offering the entrails of a ram to God for having saved him from the flood. Chronologically this episode should have come after the *Flood*, but it was painted in this position perhaps because of its small size.

The complex scene of the *Flood* was most probably the first panel to be painted by Michelangelo in December 1508. Diagonals dominate the fresco as some people take refuge under a tent, others climb onto the bits of land not yet submerged by the waters, and a small group crams onto a boat which is about to sink under the excessive weight. The multitude succumbing to the cataclysm express a wide variety of feelings: anguish, love,

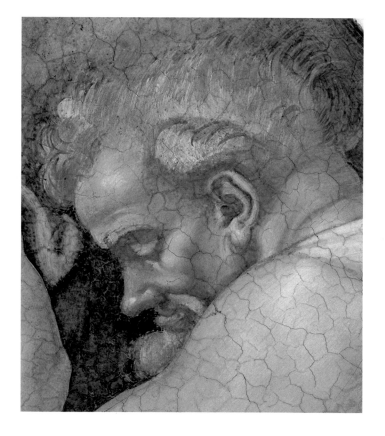

compassion and egoism, almost a foretaste of the complex human universe later to be depicted in the *Last Judgement*. Humankind tries to save itself as best it can, but is condemned to die in the natural disaster as God told Noah in the Bible: "I have determined to make an end of all flesh, for the earth is filled with violence through them. Behold, I will destroy them with the earth" (Genesis 6,13). In the centre background is the ark which, as the place of salvation, is an allegory of the Church. Noah appears at one of the windows. According to the sources, there was once a bolt of lightening (an expression of divine wrath) striking the tent on the right, but this was lost in 1797 when the plaster there collapsed following an explosion near Castel Sant'Angelo.

The last scene, the one nearest the original entrance of the chapel, shows the *Drunkenness of Noah*. The Bible recounts how Noah's three sons Ham, Japheth and Shem found him drunk. In the foreground the patriarch is lovingly covered by one of his offspring,

Sistine Chapel, Ceiling, Michelangelo,
lunette with Josias, detail
left, *lunette with Zorobabel, detail*

while the others stand talking; in the background on the left, Noah is laboriously working the land. This episode symbolizes humanity as a slave to its own vices, compelled to work as a consequence of sin.

The episodes from *Genesis* are surrounded by ten pairs of imposing male figures, the so-called *Ignudi*, whose features recall works such as the Laocoon or the Belvedere Torso. These figures, seated on blocks, looking away from the sky behind them and their agitated poses communicate a sense of deep inner unease. Their hands hold ribbons supporting medallions upon which are monochrome depictions of episodes from the Old Testament. Various critics have tried to explain the meaning of the *Ignudi* as "genii" symbolizing the pagan world, personifications of Michelangelo's neo-Platonic ideas, prisoners, wingless angels and many more, however no definitive explanation has yet been found. In terms of the composition of the fresco, the contrast with *Genesis* is evident: the panels get steadily richer in groups of characters, while the *Ignudi* remain as isolated figures, not part of a common scene but closed in the space generated by the powerful foreshortening with which they were created and

Sistine Chapel, Ceiling, Michelangelo,
Erythrean Sibyl
right, *Prophet Jeremiah*

by their own conditions of light. More isolated images are to be seen below in the twelve Seers: seven *Prophets* (Zachariah, Joel, Isaiah, Ezekiel, Daniel, Jeremiah, Jonah) recalling the Jewish tradition, and five *Sibyls* (Delphic, Erythrean, Cumaean, Persian, Lybian) recalling the Greek tradition. Together they represent those who had divine intuition. The monumental power of these figures is most striking, as is the vast assortment of colours of their clothing and the successful attempt to portray their reactions as they receive celestial revelation.

Along the outer sides of Michelangelo's fresco are the *Forerunners of Christ*: in the lunettes, the progenitors from Adam to Joseph and, in the webs, the families of Israel connected to the characters portrayed in the lunettes. The bright colours of the images stand out against the areas in shadow, following an extraordinarily modern colour scheme. Michelangelo wanted to recount the entire story of salvation and hence he chose, having told the stories of creation and sin, to recount humanity's long journey to redemption while awaiting the Redeemer.

The four spandrels at the corners of the vault represent miraculous events in which God intervened in favour of the People of Israel. The episodes, all alluding to the coming redemption by Christ, are: *Judith and Holofernese, David and Goliath*, the *Brazen Serpent* and the *Punishment of Haman*.

HIEREMIAS

The next decorative enterprises in the Sistine Chapel, dating from the time of Leo X (1513-1521), were two series of tapestries commissioned by that pope from Raphael to hang over the fake curtains at the base of the walls during solemn liturgies. The hangings were woven at the Brussels workshop of Pieter van Aelst, following drawings by Raphael. They depict the *Stories of Peter*, which were hung beneath the Old Testament cycle, and the *Stories of Paul*, placed below the frescoed scenes of the New Testament. The events from the lives of the two Princes of the Apostles were a perfect complement to the iconography already adorning the chapel, and enriched the complex effect of "discourse through images" that the pontificate sought to achieve. These precious tapestries are today kept in the Vatican Pinacoteca.

The final decorative project began in 1536 when the sixty-year-old Michelangelo, twenty-five years after completing the ceiling frescoes, began the *Last Judgement* on the end wall of the chapel. The commission had probably come two years earlier from Clement VII, but his death in 1534 meant that work only began under his successor Paul III (Alessandro Farnese 1534-1549). The fresco was officially unveiled in 1541 on the eve of All Saints. In creating this monumental *dies irae* - 200 square metres of frescoed surface with 391 figures - Michelangelo decided to abandon the combination of architecture, painting and sculpture he had earlier used on the vault. The Judgement involves the nothingness of man in the face of divine power and the artist, with great intuition, understood that architectural structures had no place there. The only architecture possible was that provided by the bodies of human beings, which still retained their heroic dimension. Here, charm and grace give way to a convulsive lack of synchronicity.
The last act in the history of salvation, the day on which human destiny is finally fulfilled, could not be ignored, and in depicting it Michelangelo drew inspiration from many sources among them, apart from the Bible, Dante's Divine Comedy.
At its completion, and even while it was still being painted, the work attracted vehement accusations of immorality from, among others, the pontifical master of ceremonies Biagio da Cesena and Pietro Aretino. The situation deteriorated in the atmosphere created by the Council of Trent, held in order to refute Protestant accusations against the Church, and eventually it was decided to cover those parts of the fresco considered obscene. In 1564, Buonarroti's pupil Daniele da Volterra, known ever since as "Braghet-

tone", was commissioned to paint "braghe" (breeches) over the nudity of Michelangelo's figures. In the recent restoration, it was decided to keep da Volterra's additions as a tangible expression of a historic era, and to remove all subsequent retouches, so that the expressive beauty of the Judgement may be enjoyed to the full.

End Wall:
"When the Son of Man comes in his glory, and all the angels with him, he will sit on his glorious throne. All the nations will be gathered before him, and he will separate people one from another as a shepherd separates the sheep from the goats. And he will place the sheep on his right, and the goats on the left. Then the King will say to those on his right, 'Come, you who are blessed by my Father, inherit the kingdom prepared for you from the foundation of the world'. (...) Then he will say to those on his left, 'Depart from me, you cursed, into the eternal fire prepared for the devil and his angels'. (...) And these will go away into eternal punishment, and the righteous into eternal life" (Mt 25, 31-46).
Michelangelo's entire composition originates in the peremptory

Sistine Chapel, end wall, Michelangelo,
Last Judgement, detail of the Virgin Mary
left, *Last Judgement*

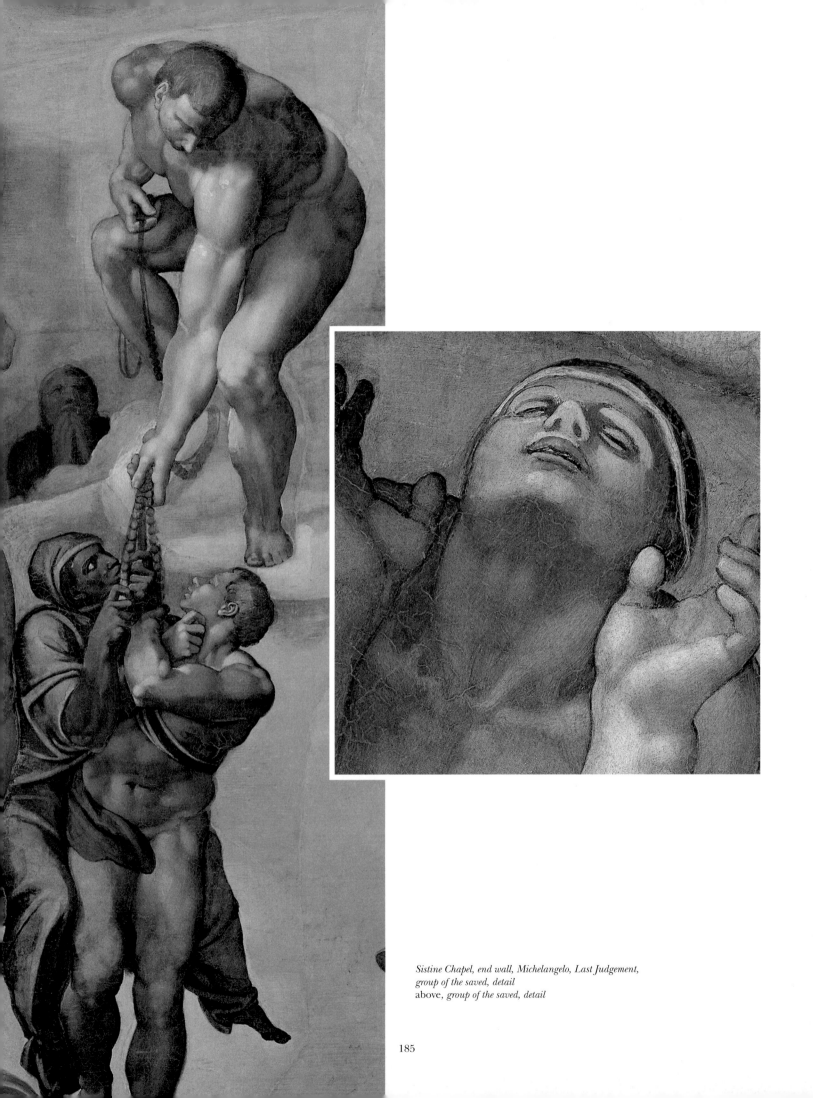

*Sistine Chapel, end wall, Michelangelo, Last Judgement,
group of the saved, detail*
above, *group of the saved, detail*

gesture of Christ the Judge who, at the top surrounded by light and accompanied by the Virgin in a pose of reigned distress, dominates the Valley of Jehoshaphat. Around Him a swirl of bodies and souls float like shipwrecked mariners adrift in the world. The painting has a concentric rhythm, its general movement recalling the rings created when a solid body falls on the smooth surface of water. In the upper section, in rigidly hierarchical order around the figure of Christ, is the celestial world with its saints, martyrs, apostles and patriarchs. Within the lunettes, groups of flying wingless angels carry the tools of the Passion: the cross, the crown of thorns and the column of flagellation. In the middle of the wall are those who, following judgement, ascend to Heaven (left), or fall to Hell (right), while in the centre a group of angels with trumpets announce the Judgement Day. At the bottom right, Charon, having carried the damned along the River Styx, pushes them towards Minos the judge of the infernal regions; on the left those who have been saved rise from death. The face of Minos is believed by some to be a likeness of Biagio da Cesena, perhaps a symbolic portrayal by the artist. Other contemporary characters are depicted in the fig-

ures of the fresco, among them the master himself. An awareness of the inevitability of the events and a sense of inadequacy are well expressed in the image of the empty skin of the Apostle Bartholomew and in the agonised self-portrait of Michelangelo which, according to most critics, it contains. It is held up as a record of his martyrdom by the figure of St Bartholomew, in whose features scholars have seen the likeness of Pietro Aretino who called for the fresco to be destroyed for its impiety. That empty lifeless skin perhaps conceals a thought that underlies the entire Judgement: the soul survives the body just as the work survives the man.

With this last enterprise of Michelangelo, the decoration of the Sistine Chapel came to an end. The Sistine Chapel - since the 17th century, the place where new popes are elected - was used, from the late 15th century, to house cardinals during conclaves. However, it must not be forgotten that its primary role is as the main chapel of the Papal Palace, used by popes to celebrate the most important religious ceremonies and feasts. It is for this reason that the greatest artists were summoned to decorate it, creating highly communicative images and giving concrete form to the unknowable.

Sistine Chapel, end wall, Michelangelo, Last Judgement,
detail of angels with long trumpets
left, *detail of St Bartholomew*

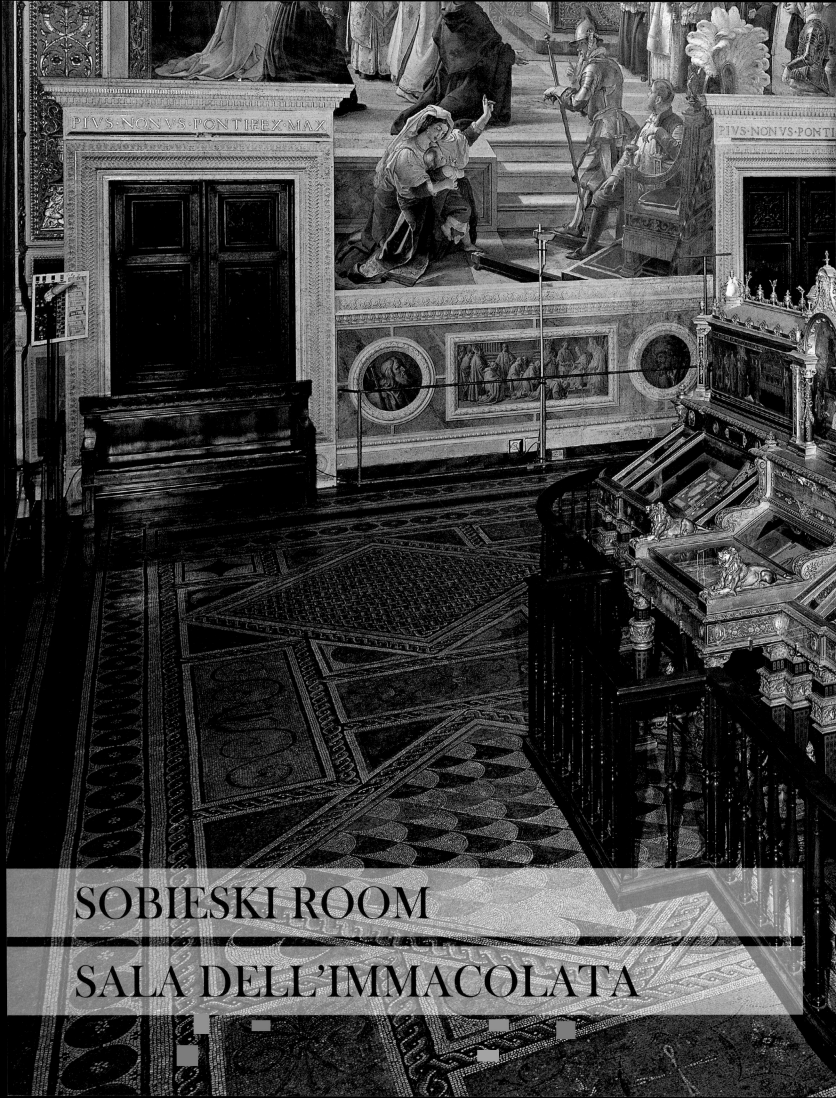

SOBIESKI ROOM

SALA DELL'IMMACOLATA

The name of the Sobieski Room comes from the large painting, *Sobieski Frees Vienna*, which covers 41 square metres on the room's northern wall. It shows the victory of the Polish King John III Sobieski over the Turks at the gates of Vienna in 1683. It is considered to be the masterpiece of Jan Matejko of Krakow, who sought the subject matter for his paintings above all in the history of his own country.

It is said that Matejko refused the agreed payment, provided the canvas be taken to Pope Leo XIII (1878-1903) for the anniversary of the second centenary of the victory of Vienna (12th September 1883).

The room also houses other works, such as *Blessed Giovanni Sarcander being led to Martyrdom* by Francesco Grandi, the *Apparition of Jesus to St Margaret Alacoque* by Francesco Podesti, *St Grata gathers the remains of St Alexander* by Ponziano Loverini, and the canvas of the *Martyrs of Gorkum* painted by Cesare Fracassini in 1867. The latter was so successful that the public flocked to see it in the artist's studio before its transfer to the Vatican.

The *Sala dell'Immacolata* (Room of the Immaculate Conception), located in the Borgia Tower, is decorated with a *cycle of frescoes dedicated to Mary Most Holy*. It was commissioned by Pope Pius IX (1846-1878) after his proclamation of the dogma of the Immaculate Conception on 8th December 1854. The pope entrusted the commission to Francesco Podesti who, by removing a floor, managed to widen the wall surfaces whereon he depicted the most important moments of that event. Atop the vault is the coat-of-arms of Pius IX and the year 1858, recalling the pope who commissioned the work and the date of its completion.

The wall facing the windows contains a striking fresco. The scene is divided into two parts, in the lower is the pope, in the middle of a large host of clergymen and nobles; in the upper is Mary, surrounded by the entire world of heaven: God the Father, the Son, the Dove representing the Holy Spirit, prophets, angels, saints and biblical characters. On the right-hand wall next to this fresco are the members of the commission that recognised the dogma, while on the left-hand wall is the scene of the crowning of the image of the Immaculate Conception over the altar of the chapel of the Choir in St Peter's.

The *Sala dell'Immacolata* also has a beautiful Roman floor from Ostia and, at its centre, a remarkable piece of furniture designed by Emile Auguste Reiber and constructed in Paris by Charles and Paul Christofle. It is made of various materials such as wood, metals, porcelain and gemstones and contains the Bull *Ineffabilis Deus* translated into all the languages of the Catholic peoples of the world, who donated it to Pius IX on 11th January 1877.

ROOM OF THE CHIAROSCURI

The Room of the Chiaroscuri is situated on the second floor of the wing of the Pontifical Palace built by Nicholas III (1277-1280). It used to be known as the room "of the Parrot" from the custom, documented by sources since the 11th century, of keeping a caged parrot in a room of the pope's apartments, something that also used to happen in his residence at Avignon. This tradition probably accounts for the probable presence of a frieze, now lost, by Giovanni da Udine, showing various animals and especially parrots. Today, by way of remembrance, two painted parrots are to be seen on either side of the entry leading to the next-door Room of the Swiss.

Also known as "of the Cubicularii" or "of the Grooms", the room was used to house both the *cubicularii secreti*, who would watch over and protect the *cubiculum* (the pope's bedroom), and the "grooms", whose duty was to carry the pontiff's *sedia gestatoria*. It also used for the ceremonial robing of the pontiff for ceremonies at the Sistine Chapel or St Peter's and, from the first half of the 16th century onwards, for secret consistory meetings of the pope and his cardinals. This latter function is what inspired the decoration commissioned by Leo X (1513-1521) from Raphael and his collaborators around 1517: the *Apostles* (with *Sts Stephen and Lawrence* added later), portrayed on the walls were ideally identified with the group of cardinals surrounding the pope, seen as Vicar of Christ. The figures in chiaroscuro - giving the room its name - are portrayed within *trompe-l'oeil* niches that alternate with fake columns. The niches are surmounted by broken cymatia with allegorical figures representing the *Virtues* flanked by *puttos* bearing festoons of flowers and fruit. At the base, twelve monochrome panels portray scenes from the lives and martyrdoms of the figures above. The room has a wooden ceiling probably made to a design by Raphael, with gold coffers that have the Medici coat-of-arms on a red background and the symbols of Leo X (the yoke, the ring and three feathers) on a blue background. In 1558 during the pontificate of Paul IV (1555-1559), the paintings were lost when it became necessary to rebuild the walls of the rooms, which were in a poor state of repair.

Two years later, Pius IV commissioned the Zuccari brothers to restore the old images. Taddeo Zuccari drew inspiration from the original scheme of apostles and saints and, according to Vasari, "having painted one, let his brother Federigo do all the rest". In reality it would seem that various artists had a hand in the project between 1560 and 1582, the year in which the restorations were completed under Gregory XIII (1572-1585).

The names most frequently associated with this phase of the work are Giovanni and Cherubino Alberti, Ignazio Danti, Cavalier d'Arpino, Pietro Santi and Pietro Camotto. Lesser interventions were undertaken by Clement XI (1700-1721), while Pius VII (1800-1823) added the five supporting pillars that divide the room into two parts; his coat-of-arms can be seen in the smaller section near the Room of Constantine. The frieze at the top of the wall was painted over various periods, on commissions from Popes Pius IV, Gregory XIII and Pius VII.

CHAPEL OF NICHOLAS V

FRA BEATO ANGELICO, ANGELICUS PICTOR

Guido di Pietro, called Fra Giovanni da Fiesole after he took the religious habit, was described by the humanist Cristoforo Landino as "angelic and charming" and by posterity as "beato" (blessed), more for the sublime concepts that inspired his works than for the establishment of his cult as being a saintly person.

His early works, while conserving the features of international Gothic, reveals an openness to the new artistic languages being developed by Masaccio, with which Fra Angelico had come into contact while an apprentice at the Carmine. His modernity resides in his being a "Christian humanist" capable of distinguishing all the elements typical of this new form of painting, such as perspective and the plastic construction of bodies. Fra Angelico's enrolment as a painter in the Company of San Niccolò al Carmine dates from 1417. The following year he entered the friary of St Dominic at Fiesole. Of him Vasari wrote: "Some say that Fra Giovanni would never have raised his brush if first he had not prayed. He never made a crucifix but his cheeks were wet with tears". In truth, the angelic artist never had to separate himself from his ecclesiastical life, except for the first year of his novitiate when he was forbidden to paint.

He is difficult to define as a painter because of his ability to analyze and combine the philosophical currents of the 15th century, the Thomist and the Neo-Platonic, and to create a form of naturalism that mediates between the historicism of Alberti and the realism of Donatello.

Where Fra Angelico's technique excelled was in the use of light, suffusing the painted surface and giving a sense of unity to the scenes. This vivid light, mystically interpreted, becomes almost a divine emanation that optimizes the colours, the brilliance of which is also due to the use of gold. Giulio Carlo Argan said that "Piero della Francesca started from this point to achieve that fusion of space and light which is the synthesis of all the great themes of art in the 15th century: the search for human and divine knowledge, for a form capable of expressing equally well the drama and contrast of human life, and the eternal and rational laws of nature".

Chapel of Nicholas V, Fra Angelico, St Stephen giving alms, detail

Located in the 13th century tower of Innocent III (1198-1216), one of the oldest parts of the Pontifical Palace, the Chapel of Nicholas V is dedicated to Sts Martyrs Stephen and Lawrence and is so called because it was the private chapel of Nicholas V (Tommaso Parentucelli 1447-1455). It has a rectangular plan with a cross vault and pilasters on the walls. Light comes from two narrow arched windows and a lunette over the altar.

Nicholas V's coat-of-arms is in a circle situated in the centre of the dichromate marble floor. The original entrance, now walled up, was from a passageway near the present entrance which was commissioned by Julius II (1503-1513). Gregory XIII (1572-1585) created another entrance below the scene of the martyrdom of St Lawrence, of which part of the plaster fell during the work.

Despite its small size, the chapel has a cycle of wall paintings unanimously recognised as a real art treasure, commissioned from Fra Angelico directly by the pope in 1447.

The work, completed with the collaboration of Benozzo Gozzoli, is the only fresco cycle documenting the painter's presence in Rome. The artist worked on the decoration until the end of 1451, replacing a series of pre-existing frescoes dating from the time of Nicholas III (1277-1280).

In the webs of the vault are the four *Evangelists* against a starry background. The stories of the martyrs Stephen and Lawrence are to be seen on three sides of the room: on three of the lunettes on the lower part of the vault are six scenes from the life of St Stephen (the *Saint receiving the diaconate from St Peter* and the *Saint giving alms, St Stephen's Sermon* and the *Disputation in the Sanhedrin, St Stephen being led to Martyrdom* and his *Stoning*).

Underneath are five rectangular frescoes dedicated to St Lawrence (*St Sixtus bestowing the diaconate on St Lawrence, St Sixtus giving St Lawrence the treasure of the Church, St Lawrence giving alms to the Poor, St Lawrence appearing before Emperor Decius* and the *Martyrdom of St Lawrence*). A series of damask curtains runs along the base.

In the window embrasures are paintings of *Rosettes, Heads of Prophets, Patriarchs* and of *Christ*, while eight *Saints and Fathers of the Church* are depicted on the pilasters. On the end wall, over the altar, was an altarpiece of a *Deposition* by Fra Angelico, now lost.

Chapel of Nicholas V, Fra Angelico, St Thomas
left, *Saint Sixtus bestowing the diaconate on St Lawrence*
pages 192 and 193, *Fra Angelico, St Stephen receiving the diaconate from St Peter* and *St Stephen giving alms*

These frescoes date from a particularly important period in the development of Fra Angelico's style. Indeed, both his style and his artistic ideas were changed and enriched with his arrival in Rome and his consequent exposure to the refined cultural world surrounding Nicholas V, a distinguished scholar and bibliophile strongly linked to the humanistic movement.

The new concept of perspective here takes on a concrete form. Fra Angelico used his brush to emphasise the sacred nature of these images, setting them within typically Roman architecture. In the scene where St Stephen receives his diaconate from St Peter, the imposing edifice, the monumental figures and their calm gestures caused Giulio Carlo Argan to remark that here Angelico gave life to his "Latin sermons". Indeed, these stories restore a humanistic aspect to early Christianity, above all through the pictorial reconstruction of ancient Roman architecture.

This is the lesson that should be drawn from the art in the Chapel of Nicholas V, which the papacy used as a means of underlining its own power. It should not be forgotten that these frescos were part of a wider and more complex design of Nicholas V who undertook the transformation of the *Urbe* - a preparatory step before the later interventions of Sixtus IV (1471-1484).

V. L'Evangelizzazione americana vista dall'Europa del sec. XVI

MUSEUMS OF THE
VATICAN LIBRARY

With its innumerable manuscripts, parchments, drawings, engravings, autographs, incunabula and printed books, the Vatican Apostolic Library is considered to be one of the world's major collections.

According to the sources, the Roman Church began collecting books from its earliest days. Indeed it is certain that the Lateran *Patriarchio* contained the ancient *scrinium sanctum*, the archive and library of the pontiffs, placed under the protection of St Lawrence.

In the Middle Ages these libraries would follow the popes as they moved from one to another of their chosen residences and gradually, due also to historical and political upheavals, the collections were dispersed. The present Vatican Apostolic Library was conceived by the humanist Pope Nicholas V (1447-1455) who intended it *pro communi doctorum virorum commodo*, that is, for the use of scholars and not only *ad usum Pontificis*. The original nucleus of texts, including Latin and Greek codices, was soon augmented by new manuscripts which Nicholas himself ordered to be copied. His project, however, remained in the planning stages and was only implemented during the pontificate of Sixtus IV (1471-1484) who, with the Bull *Ad decorem militantis ecclesiae* of 15th June 1475, formally instituted the library, assigning it rooms on the ground floor of the north wing of the Palace of Nicholas V. Access was through

the Courtyard of the "Pappagallo". The pope made the library financially independent by granting it private revenues and appointed a librarian, Bartolomeo Sacchi known as Platina, as documented in Melozzo da Forlì's famous fresco of 1477 in a room of the library, today preserved in the Vatican Pinacoteca.

By 1589 the space had become insufficient and Pope Sixtus V (1585-1590) had the library moved and placed in a new building, a transversal arm designed by Domenico Fontana on the opposite side of the Belvedere Courtyard. It proved to be a good move because from there the *Libraria* could expand along the west arm of the courtyard.

Over the following centuries transformations took place that increased the volume of the library, particularly thanks to the acquisition policy put into effect by later pontiffs, who managed to acquire various important book collections and private archives. In addition to this, and especially from the 18th century onwards, were antiquarian collections and a considerable number of true works of art, all kept in the Library Museums which, on 1st October 1999, passed to the jurisdiction of the Vatican Museums.

The library currently has thirteen exhibition rooms. The Address Hall of Pius IX, dating from 1877, was so-called because it was used to keep copies of the addresses of homage sent to the pope from all over the world; today it contains *Byzantine cloths and liturgical vestments*. The Chapel of St Pius V, from the second half of the 16th cen-

Vatican Apostolic Library,
View of Urban VIII's Gallery
left, *View of the Sistine Hall*

tury and decorated with *Stories from the life of St Peter the Martyr* by Jacopo Zucchi to drawings by Vasari, is today designated to house the *Treasure of the Sancta Sanctorum*. The Address Hall was used in the past to display Byzantine icons and works of the "primitives"; under Pius XI (1922-1939) it was used to keep the addresses of homage sent to Leo XIII (1878-1903) and St Pius X (1903-1914) by the faithful from all over the world. It currently houses Roman and early-Christian glassware, and *enamels, ivories* and *metals* dating from the Middle Ages to the Modern Age. The Room of the Aldobrandini Marriage was built during the pontificate of Paul V (1605-1621) by the architect Flaminio Ponzio and decorated by Guido Reni with a cycle on

the *Stories of Samson*. It derives its name from the famous Augustan fresco of a wedding scene that once belonged to Cardinal Pietro Aldobrandini. The next room, known as the Room of the Papyri, was created during the time of Clement XIV (1769-1774) for the 6th and 7th-century *papyri* of Ravenna. It was decorated under Pius VI (1775-1799) by Mengs, who did the *Allegory of History* on the vault, while Christopher Unterberger did the ornamental decorations and cornices. The *Museo Sacro* (Museum of Christian Art) was founded by Pope Benedict XIV (1740-1758) to house early Christian finds The ceiling has the *Triumph of the Church* and the *Triumph of Faith* painted by Stefano Pozzi in 1757. Among the objects on display are sev-

HIC·TRIA·SIXTE·TVO·CAPITI·DIADEMATA·DANTVR
SED·QVARTVM·IN·CAELIS·TE·DIADEMA·MANET

eral *oil-lamps*, a mosaic *travel icon* from the 12th-13th century showing *St Theodore*, and the "*aquamanile*" used, according to tradition, by St Lawrence to administer baptism. Next comes the Gallery of Urban VIII, restored and furnished by that pope in 1624, and the Sistine Rooms built by Domenico Fontana at the time of Sixtus V to keep documents from the papal archives. The grand and imposing Sistine Hall, also named for Sixtus V who conceived it as a reading room, has wall decorations depicting the most famous *libraries of antiquity* and the *Ecumenical Councils* that most concerned themselves with books, as well as *views of Rome* documenting the pontiff's interventions there. The two Pauline Rooms were added at the time of Paul

V to house Greek manuscripts. The Alexandrine Room was created in 1690 by Alexander VIII (1689-1691). The vast Clementine Gallery dates from the time of Clement XII (1730-1740). The last area, the Profane Museum of the Library, is due to Clement XIII (1758-1769) and contains various Etruscan and Roman objects.

Vatican Apostolic Library, Sistine Hall,
Parade for the Crowning of Sixtus V
left, *St Peter's Square at the time of Sixtus V*

GREGORIAN PROFANE MUSEUM

The collection in the Gregorian Profane Museum includes various antiquities, mainly from excavations undertaken in the pontifical territories in the early 19th century. This collection, created by Gregory XVI (1831-1846) in 1844, was originally located in the Lateran Palace. It was transferred to the Vatican by order of John XXIII (1958-1963) but only inaugurated in 1970. A marble bust of Gregory XVI may be seen on the right of the museum entrance, in memory of the founder.

The works have been arranged according to rigorous philological criteria, and with the aim of removing arbitrary additions and later restorations. The five sections of the museum include Greek originals, Roman imperial copies, Roman republican and early-imperial sculptures, urns, sarcophagi, funerary altars and 2nd-3rd-century Roman sculptures.

There is no doubt that Greek art laid down the aesthetic norms and canons which have remained as a constant reference for the subsequent evolution of western art.

A *Head of Athena*, dating from around 460 BC and ascribable to the cultural environment of Magna Graecia, was once part of an acrolith, an archaic type of statue where limbs and head were made of precious materials like marble and ivory and the rest of the body with other materials, such as wood covered with sheets of precious metal. The most famous example is the chryselephantine statue of Athena in the Parthenon, a work by Phidias. This head is

embellished with various insertions: chalcedony for the eyeballs, bronze strips for the eyelashes and glass paste for the pupils, no longer in place.

Also worthy of note is the *memorial stele of a young man* dating from about 450 BC. It shows the youth in the act of saying farewell, while another young boy is holding out a strigil and an oil flask.

Among fragments from the sculptural friezes of the Parthenon is a horse's head from the western pediment. The pediment was destroyed in 1687 but, as we can infer from a drawing by Jacques Carrey in 1674, it depicted the dispute between Athena and Poseidon for the rule of Attica. The fragment in the Vatican Museums belonged to the front horse of Athena's chariot. A fragment with the *head of a young boy* is from a relief on the northern frieze of the Parthenon showing the procession of the Panathenaea, feasts celebrated every four years in honour of Athena. A *bearded head*, probably King Erichthonius of Athens, was originally on the southern side of the Parthenon, in one of ninety-two metopes showing mythological battle scenes.

Among the Roman copies is a sculptural group with *Athena and*

Gregorian Profane Museum,
fragment of the head of Athena completed in plaster
left, *View of the Museum*

Marsyas the original of which, attributed to Myron, was made in the mid 5th century BC as a votive offering for the acropolis of Athens. The original appearance of the group is known thanks to the literary record of Pausanias and Pliny and to depictions on coins of the period. According to the myth, the satyr, a spirit of waters and mountains, picked up a flute discarded by Athena and soon became the most popular player among the followers of the Goddess Cybele. Apollo was jealous, not accepting that his pre-eminence as god of music be disputed. He challenged Marsyas and after having beaten him, punished the satyr for his pride by having him flayed. Myron's Marsyas is shown as he suddenly starts back when the goddess forbids him to take the flute. The perfection and realism with which the artist caught the moment provide a foretaste of the typical characteristics of classical Greek sculpture.

The museum also has a *Head of Sophocles.* This sculpture, found in Terracina in 1839, is considered by critics to be a copy of the original commissioned by Jophon, son of the great Greek tragic poet. It is not, then, a copy of the other portrait of Sophocles mentioned in the sources, which was ordered by Lycurgus, together with those of Aeschylus and Euripides, to put on display in the Theatre of Dionysus in Athens.

Also in this section is the *Chiaramonti Niobid,* discovered in the 16th century near Villa Adriana in Tivoli. It is probably a Roman copy of a 2nd-century BC Hellenistic group showing one of the daughters of Niobe, the wife of King Amphion of Thebes, as she desperately tries to avoid the deadly arrows shot by Apollo and Artemis in response to the offence caused by Niobe to their mother Latona. This is confirmed by Pliny the Elder who claims that the original, which also included the mother and sisters, was probably made by Scopas or Praxiteles. In this sculpture the effect of movement is achieved

though the folds of the chiton and the mantle around the hips of the solitary Niobid.

The section dedicated to Roman sculptures from the 1st and early 2nd centuries contains fragments discovered in 1939 under the *Palazzo della Cancelleria,* part of a frieze from the base of an altar or sculpture. These reliefs - conventionally known as the *Altar* or the *Base of the Vicomagistri* - show a procession made up of two figures dressed in togas (with three lictors behind them), two assistants, three trumpeters, a number of *victimarii* pushing an ox, a bull and a cow, and other figures also wearing togas, among them four *pueri riciniati.* The scene, considered to be a sacrificial procession involving the *magistri vici,* probably dates from the age of Tiberius. It is interesting to note how the figures are linked to one another through their various poses in an attempt at spatial unification.

The museum also has certain slabs - found in 1939 under the *Palazzo della Cancelleria* and probably once part of a triumphal arch - known as the *Domitian Reliefs.* The first shows the *Departure of Domitian:* the

Gregorian Profane Museum,
Altar or Base of the Vicomagistri
right, *relief of the sepulchre of the Haterii, detail*

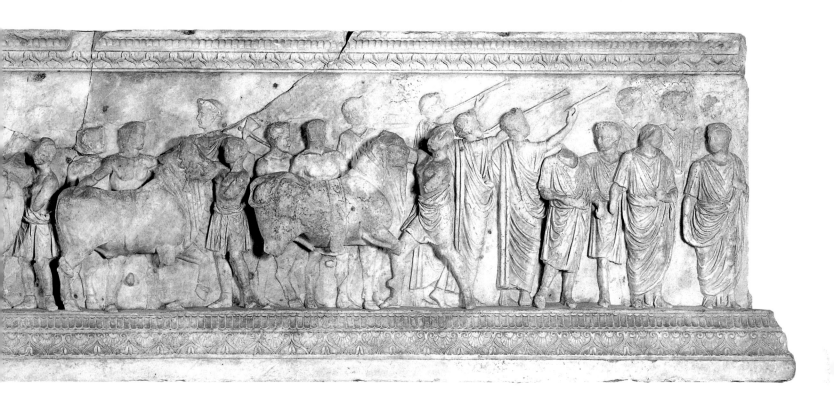

ARCVSINSACRAVIASVMMA

emperor, preceded by a winged Victory, two lictors, Mars and Minerva, is guided by the goddess Virtus who holds him by the arm. Following the emperor are the two Genii of the Senate and people of Rome, four praetorians, and other lictors in the background. The second relief represents the *Arrival of Vespasian*: on the left, near the statue of the goddess Roma, five vestals are escorted by a lictor, while on the right the emperor, wearing the crown of Victory, is received by his son Domitian behind whom the two Genii again appear. The first episode is perhaps to be linked to the campaign against the Germans of 83 AD; the second possibly shows Domitian who, having saved Rome, restores it to his father.

Another relief, depicting five ancient Roman monuments, documents the construction of certain important buildings from the Flavian age. This frieze is part of a series of finds held by the museum that were taken from the *Tomb of the Haterii*, which stood at the third mile of the Via Labicana. It depicts: the arch marking the entrance of the Temple of Isis (*Iseo Campese*) built just after 80 AD, the Coliseum still without its top storey, a four-sided arch, the Arch of Titus, and the Temple of Jupiter Custos enlarged about 90 AD. Presumably, the dead man was a contractor who had had an active role in the construction of the buildings shown.

The collection also has a section dedicated to *sarcophagi*. Outstanding among them are those depicting mythological subjects such as the stories of Hercules, Adonis, Phaedra and Hippolytus, Orestes, the Niobids, Mars and Rhea Silvia, Selene and Endymion.

Among examples of 2nd and 3rd-century Roman sculpture are a porphyry *torso of a cuirassed statue* found in 1869 near the hospital of St John Lateran, an excellent work portraying an emperor, probably Trajan or Hadrian; a statue with a *head-portrait of Omphale*, queen of Lydia; and the *statue of Aesculapius*, characterized by his stick encircled by a snake.

Brief mention must also be made of the pagan epigraphic collection, currently located in the Gregorian Museum and only open to scholars. It was originally part of the Lateran Museum where it was catalogued by Giovanni Battista de Rossi in 1900 and arranged in subject order by Orazio Marucchi.

Gregorian Profane Museum, group of statues from the excavations of Cerveteri

PIO-CHRISTIAN MUSEUM

The collection held in the Pio-Christian Museum was originally on display in the Lateran Palace but was later transferred to the Vatican, as was the case with the Gregorian Profane and Ethnological Missionary Museums, by order of John XXIII (1958-1963). The exhibition area, located in a new wing of the Vatican Museums, was opened to the public on 15th June 1970.

The old Lateran Christian Museum was founded by Pius IX (Giovanni Maria Mastai Ferretti 1846-1878) in 1854, two years after the foundation of the Pontifical Commission for Sacred Archaeology which had the task of supervising excavations in the catacombs and early Christian monuments of the city. The collection included a large number of sculptures, arranged by the Jesuit Fr. Giuseppe Marchi, and an outstanding collection of epigraphs catalogued by Giovanni Battista de Rossi.

The exhibits - mostly sarcophagi - are arranged according to chronology, typology and iconography, thus offering a broad overview of the early Christian art that developed, above all, following the Edict of Milan in 313 AD by which Emperor Constantine had granted freedom of worship to the followers of the new faith.

Late antiquity saw the birth of a different artistic language, at once autonomous yet deeply permeated by the atmosphere of late-imperial Rome.

The subjects are often taken from ancient art but are imbued with new meanings. For example Orpheus becomes a "figure" of Christ, while Adonis or Endymion lend themselves to the depiction of Jonah lying under his booth. Moreover, characters are rendered using different formal procedures and the figures, while retaining an aesthetic value, have a symbolic meaning and a message to convey. Thus a new art of communication by signs was born, an art conveying Christian concepts through image-symbols.

Among the most famous works in the collection is the statue of the *Good Shepherd*, originally part of a sarcophagus. This 5th-century sculpture, much restored in the 18th century, represents a beardless young man with long curly hair wearing a short tunic

and carrying a lamb across his shoulders. The image, which recalls the ancient figure of the shepherd "criophorus" ("carrying a lamb"), ideally evokes John's words, "I am the good shepherd. The good shepherd lays down his life for his sheep" (John 10,11). In early Christian art the shepherd represented Christ the Saviour. A further reference may be traced to the gospel parable of the lost sheep.

On the front of the *Sarcophagus of Sabinus*, dating from around 315, are episodes taken from the New Testament and from apocryphal accounts of the life of the Apostle Peter. The composition has groups of figures forming various narrative nuclei, lined homogeneously around the central image of a praying woman flanked by the standing figures of Peter and Paul. These are miraculous scenes and as such represent an announcement of the salvation to be wrought by divine intervention, which is visibly evoked in the woman's posture, her raised hands in prayer and invocation.

Also part of this collection is the so-called *dogmatic sarcophagus* dating from between 325 and 350. The front is decorated with scenes from the Old and New Testaments on two levels. Included in the upper level are the couple for whom the sarcophagus was made, portrayed inside a *clipeus*. It should be noted that this is the oldest depiction of the Trinity that creates man.

The same kind of composition as found in the previous example is used on the *sarcophagus of two brothers*. It dates from about 350 and has an interesting peculiarity: one of the two male figures to whom the tomb belongs is wearing female clothes. This demonstrates how such sarcophagi were mass-produced, roughly finished in the workshops, and only given the final touches when the need arose. This sarcophagus, evidently made for a couple, was modified to accommodate two brothers, but in his hurry the mason slipped up.

Nonetheless, the sarcophagus stands out as a masterpiece for its excellent workmanship and style, and the figures are striking for their powerful three-dimensionality and the formal care with which they were sculpted.

Pio-Christian Museum,
graffito representing Jonah and the Pistrice
left, *Good Shepherd*
pages 208 and 209, *an area in the museum*

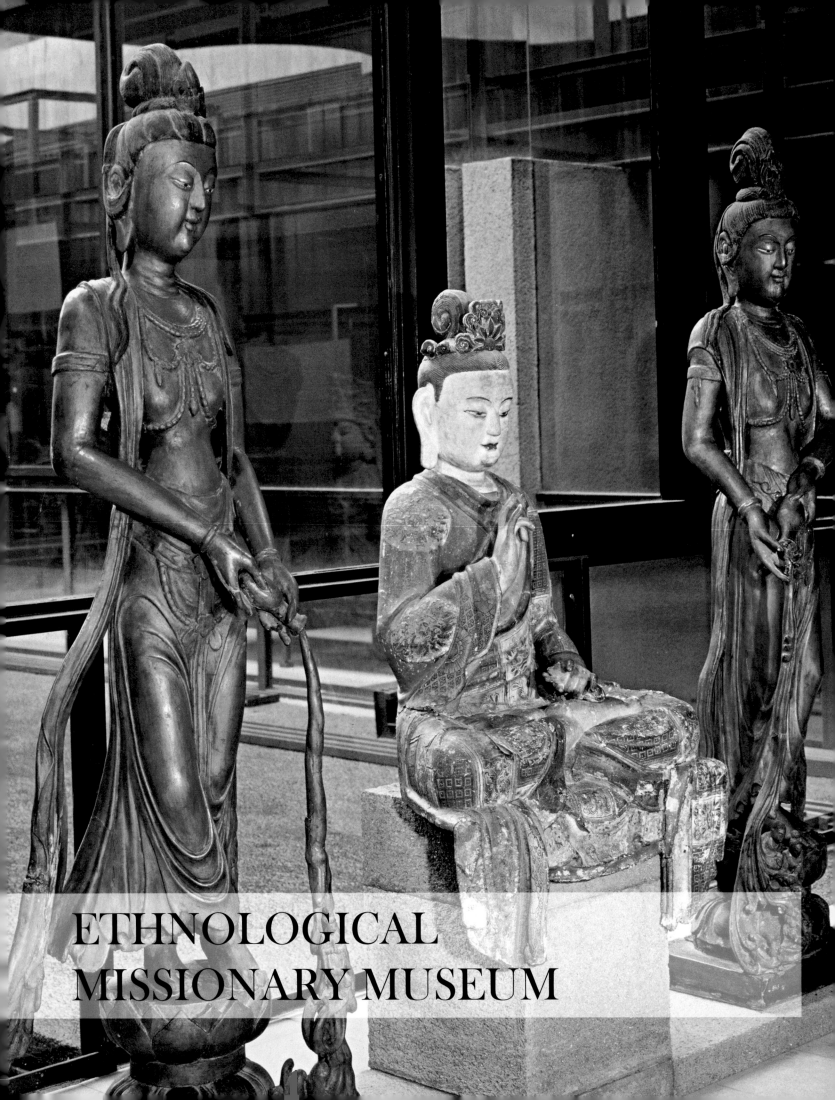

ETHNOLOGICAL
MISSIONARY MUSEUM

The Ethnological Missionary Museum was established by Pius XI (1922-1939) on 12th November 1926 at the end of the Universal Missionary Exhibition of the Holy Year 1925. Originally in the Lateran Palace, it was moved to its present site by John XXIII (1958-1963) and inaugurated by Paul VI (1963-1978) in 1973. The collection consists of works from all over the world brought together for the 1925 exhibition, objects from the Borgia Museum and from various private collections. It constitutes a valuable record of the cultural, socio-economic and religious aspects of non-European civilisations.

The main itinerary of the museum follows a geo-cultural arrangement and is subdivided into five sections: Asia, Oceania, Africa and America, with an additional sector called "Missionary Synthesis" containing works produced following widespread evangelisation by the Church in various parts of the world. A further collection, open only to scholars, contains articles belonging to ethnographical collections.

The first section concerns the religious cultures of Asia. Among objects from China is a polychrome wooden sculpture of *Buddha Vairochana*, represented in the typical lotus position while "starting" the law wheel. A number of paintings of the *Martyrs of Nagasaki of 1597* are from Japan, the work of Okayama Shunkyo in 1927.

In the section dedicated to art from Oceania is a noteworthy wooden carving from Mangareva Island depicting the god Tu. He, according to local tradition, is the benefactor of humanity. From Easter Island we have a *figure of Moai Kavakava ancestor* (a deity and dispenser of knowledge to whom ritual dances and ceremonies were dedicated), characterised by the skeletal definition of the carving on the chest. The

Ceremonial House of Men is from New Guinea. It is a sacred hut, known as a "tambaran" and dedicated to the cult of ancestors, where male initiation rites took place. Entry to the House of Men was forbidden to women and children.

The section dedicated to Africa contains various exhibits: drapes, fragments of vases, objects from Islamic culture, earthenware figures and amulets, as well as ceremonial masks, some complete with costumes and musical instruments. These include an *agbogho monnwu helmet face mask* from Nigeria, belonging to the Igbo people.

From the American continent is a stone carving representing the Mexican divinity *Quetzalcoatl*, the Plumed Serpent, considered by the Aztecs to be the god of Wind. Among countless other works, the museum also possesses a collection of bust portraits of members of North America Indian tribes, the work of Ferdinand Pettrich, a pupil of the Danish Bertel Thorvaldsen, and donated to Pius IX by the artist himself.

The last section of the museum contains objects of Christian art produced in the mission lands; articles deriving from the meeting of different cultures where Christian themes are absorbed and translated into the style and taste of eastern civilisation. Representative examples include an ink painting on white silk showing the *Last Supper* by Chinese artist Wang-Su-Ta; and another painting on silk, the *Introduction of Christianity to Japan*, depicting the arrival of St Francis Xavier, the martyrdom of Nagasaki and the Virgin Mary as queen of Japan, work of the Japanese artist Luca Hasegawa.

Ethnological Missionary Museum,
Wang-Su-Ta, Last Supper
left, *statue of Buddha flanked by two Taoist divinities*

COLLECTION OF MODERN RELIGIOUS ART

Figurative art has always been the expression of an artist's soul, a means to communicate thoughts, sensations, ideologies and whatever else he or she wished to convey. Of all the subjects tackled over the centuries, the sacred has undoubtedly been the driving force and stimulus behind much artistic production. Artists who lived last century, though they may have chosen to express their spirituality with different materials and forms from those used in the past, are no exception. Modern art has shown itself capable of depicting faith, its methods unprecedented, extreme, abrasive, yet evocative of the present.

It is to Paul VI (1963-1978), with his profound awareness of the potential of such art, that the Collection of Modern Religious Art is due. During a homily in 1964, he urged contemporary artists to express their religious feelings using their own methods and language: "We must leave to your voices that free and powerful song of which you are capable", he said. The huge response to the pope's call took concrete form in a rich series of donations that went to enlarge the origi-

nal nucleus of modern works of art, formed in the Vatican between 1956 and 1957 by order of Pius XII (1939-1958). That collection, of about thirty works, constituted the section of modern art in the Pinacoteca, but as it grew larger it was moved to a new independent exhibition area consisting of rooms specially built under the Sistine Chapel, in the Borgia Tower and Apartment and in the so-called Borgia *Salette*. The museum, comprising painting, sculpture, graphic art, and some stained glass, was inaugurated in 1973. A walk through the opulent Vatican collection gives the observer a global view of a dense and multifaceted universe including artists, languages and movements from the late 19th to the late 20th century. The original nucleus included works by Rouault, Utrillo, Villon, Zadkine, Rodin, Fazzini, Guidi, Greco, Messina, Sironi, Previati, Mancini, Puccinelli, De Chirico, Carrà, Soffici, Tosi, De Pisis, Morandi, Viani, Rosai, Arturo Martini and others. Over the years, other names have been added to enlarge the collection.

Modern Religious Art Collection,
Room XII, Mario Radice, Christ in the Garden
left, *Room XVI, Vincent Van Gogh, Pietà*
pages 214 and 215, *Room XV, Georges Rouault, Automne ou Nazareth*

The Collection of Modern Religious Art has no obligatory route dictated by history, contents or the exhibition space, only, perhaps, by logistics. Many routes, many systems, are possible. The spectator enjoys an aesthetic experience in which the multiform richness of 20th-century styles becomes an entrance to a world made up of rhythms and colours transposed in the spirituality of religion.

An approach to this sacred art might begin from one of the life-size *studies* executed by Henri Matisse between 1948 and 1949 for the *chapelle du Rosaire* in Vence. In 1947 the artist had agreed to concern himself with the architecture and decoration, as well as the furnishings and liturgical vestments, of the oratory of Dominican nuns, planning a simple structure in order to exalt the decorative elements. In a letter to Laurens, Matisse writes, "I have to juggle to maintain an expressive balance between two forces: the colour of the glass on the right, and the black and white on the whole left side". Attracted as he was by the Byzantine world, and particularly by the effect of reflected light, Matisse designed yellow, green and blue stained-glass windows with vegetal motifs, which let the luminous rays filter through to the irregular surfaces of the facing ceramic panels, generating soft pearly shades. In that colourful reflection, he had found the *trait d'union* for the entire composition. The artist entrusted the semantic meaning of his whole production to the scenes – St Dominic, the Virgin and Child and the Via Crucis – painted in black and white on ceramic walls. A comparison between the study for the image of the Virgin, displayed here, and the real work, testifies to the passage from an original Byzantine-like figure to one with Chinese characteristics. For the eighty-two-year-old master of Cateau Cambrésis, Vence was "the last goal of a whole life devoted to work", as he himself wrote in a book on the chapel.

Mario Sironi, a fervent advocate of a return to traditional Italian painting, has a number of his works from various periods on display in the Vatican Museums. The imposing nature of the artist's images derives from a process of geometric reduction of form and from their solid plasticity. In *Conversation: the disciples*, a work in oil on paper from 1936, the three figures impose themselves upon the scene with a monumental quality typical of megaliths. The material itself is rough and unrefined, almost like cave paintings. Solem-

Modern Religious Art Collection, Room VII,
Henri Matisse, Virgin with Child, detail

nity is rendered by an immobile sense of suspended time, confining the characters within the physical limits of the painting itself.

Francesco Messina's reliefs on the *Horrors of War* were donated to the collection in 1994. They are a series of bronzes echoing Goya's famous cycle of engravings on the *Disasters of the War* that condemned the senseless crimes caused by the French invasion. The Sicilian sculptor has created scenes in which emotion is communicated through the essence of narrative.

An outstanding exponent and theorist of late 19th-century Italian divisionism, Gaetano Previati's painting is characterised by strong elements of symbolism, filtered by his study and admiration of the French painter Odilon Redon. His application of colour, impressed in filaments upon the canvas, and the fierce backlighting of his figures and landscapes, generate a mysterious and disturbing enchantment. Fourteen of his canvases that form a highly evocative cycle on the *Via Crucis* are on display here.

The collection also includes works by Renato Guttuso: two oils, *The Coliseum* (1972) and the *Hand of the Crucified Christ* (1965); a charcoal drawing on paper of a theme taken from the *Triumph of Death* in Palazzo Sclafani; and two studies of the *Crucifixion*. Although attracted by social painting, and aiming at a realistic art of civil commitment, Guttuso did not shrink from tackling subjects taken from the Christian religious spirit (consider his famous 1941 *Crucifixion* in the National Gallery of Modern Art in Rome). His openness to Expressionist influences is visible, above all in the third of the abovementioned works in the Vatican Museums, where the image is intensified by the stroke superimposed on the figures, crossing and binding them.

Bringing the divine to a human scale seems to be the aim pursued by Georges Rouault, one of the main 20th-century painters of sacred art. Well represented in the Vatican collection, above all with the etchings and aquatints of the *Miserere* cycle, and the canvas *Automne ou Nazareth* of 1948, the Parisian Rouault presented his religious commitment in a typically modern way, far removed from the laudatory realism of sacred painting in the previous century. "Peace rarely seems to reign over this world tormented by shadows and appearances", wrote the artist, admirably summing

Modern Religious Art Collection,
Graham Sutherland, Study for Crucifixion

up the moral degradation into which modern society had fallen. Rouault's forms and his peculiar methods, almost akin to glass painting (something he had tried in his youth), give his art a constant and singular quality that is both decorative and deeply speculative.

The Collection of Modern Religious Art also has a painting by Van Gogh dating from 1890, the year of the famous Dutch artist's death. It is a *Pietà*, a copy of a work by Delacroix as indicated in the autograph note on the bottom right ("*d'après Eug Delacroix a apartenu à Diaz*"). It is a typical example of Van Gogh's style: bright colours, agitated movement and rapid brushstrokes that seem to follow the power of the mind rather than of real life. This work was donated to the museum by the archdiocese of New York.

The collection contains six works by Marc Chagall. "When I paint the wings of an angel, they are also flames, thoughts or desires...", wrote the artist summing up his "feelings" in a phrase that transcends symbolism and surrealism. Historical events experienced in a dream state, typical of the painter from Vitebsk, take concrete form in the fine *gouache* of *Le Christ et le peintre* (*L'artiste et son Modéle*), dated 1951, in which the master sought to represent the inspiration he felt while contemplating the crucifix. Christ on the cross is surrounded by angels and the artist himself is depicted in the place usually occupied by the pious women.

A number of cityscapes by Maurice Utrillo, the "accursed painter", bear witness to the Parisian artist's personal reflections on the unavoidable sufferings in life. Through his paintings, the Bard of Montmartre - the area where he was born and where, alternating with periods in mental asylums, he lived - highlights the alienation of his psychological state. His scenes are dominated by mostly-empty streets, occupied at most by solitary men and women, and surrounded by imposing buildings and churches. The Vatican collection contains, among other works, his *Sacred Heart*, a painting on cardboard from 1945.

Silence reigns in the works of Giorgio Morandi. Living far from the cultural atmosphere of his times and from the fervour of avant-garde art, the Bolognese artist, through the few everyday objects that constitute the material of his poetic universe, creates

Modern Religious Art Collection, Room XVII, Maurice Utrillo, Sacred Heart
pages 224 and 225, *Room L, Fernando Botero,*
Journey towards the Ecumenical Council

Modern Religious Art Collection, Room XLVI, Salvador Dalì,
Angelic Landscape
above, *Angelic Landscape, detail*

227

an opaque and muted atmosphere of immense lyrical abstraction. The collection includes a series of drawings of flowers, landscapes and still lives, including the *Landscape with a Farmhouse* from 1935 and the *Italian Still Life* of 1957.

There are a number of works by De Chirico, three on religious subjects, a view of the Duomo of Milan, four still lives, a tempera entitled *Mannequins* and a *Piazza of Italy*. His dreamlike flights take solid shape in the narration of episodes from Holy Scripture, such as the *Conversion of St Paul* from 1946 in which the spiritual quest is expressed through a form of painting that has its reference and origin in Renaissance art. His dramatic temperament fuses with this intelligent and grandiose manner of painting, and his pleasure in narrating is evident in the dense sky, the opulent characters and the splendid, burning and intense colours.

The collection contains two works paradigmatic of the translation of religious themes into the language of new art forms: *Study for Crucifixion* by Graham Sutherland, and *Study for Velázquez Pope II* by Francis Bacon. It is no coincidence that the same exhibition area also contains two ceramics decorated by Picasso, the artist who, through his lessons on the deconstruction of the figure, gave a powerful impulse that led to the separation between artistic representation and real appearance.

The *Crucifixion* by Sutherland is, in its own way, a symbol of the return to figurative painting; or rather it is an example of how such painting has been transformed following the novelties introduced by the avant-garde. Painted fourteen years after the *Crucifixion*, Bacon's work, in modifying an icon of art such as Velázquez's *Innocent X*, reiterates this fundamental change in art history and the new freedom offered to painters.

Modern Religious Art Collection,
Room XXV, Giorgio De Chirico, Conversion of St Paul
left, Room XVI, Marc Chagall, Christ and the Painter

Gregorian Etruscan Museum, Room XIX, Bernardino Nocchi (?), Simonetti Staircase

ARTISTS MENTIONED

POPES MENTIONED

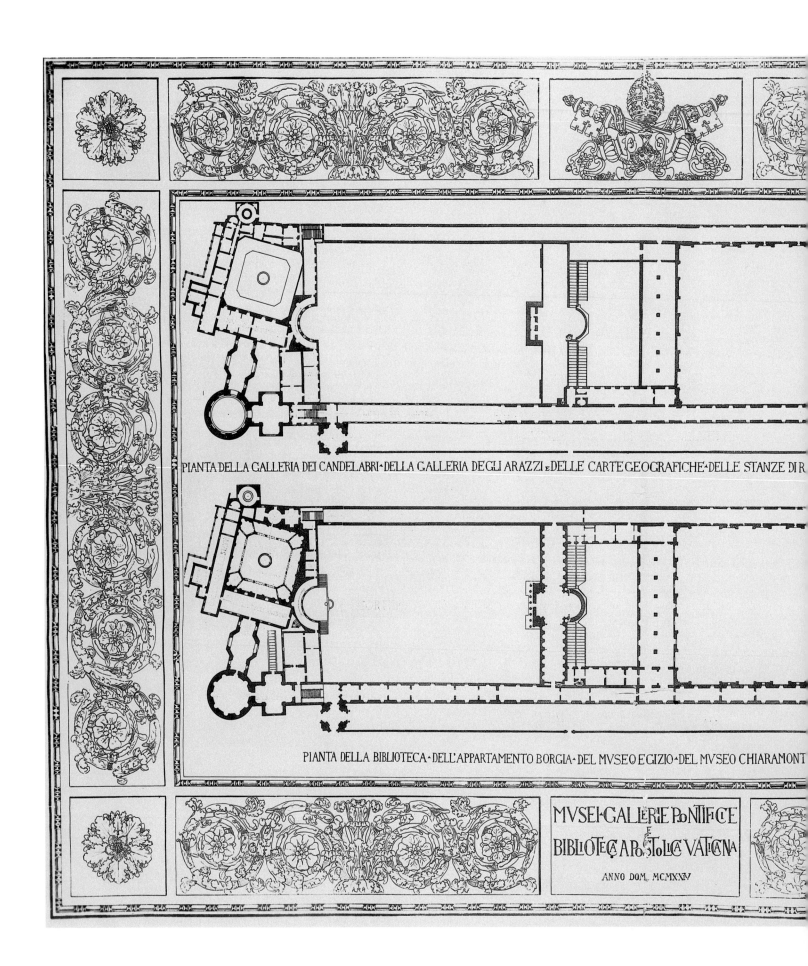

PIANTA DELLA GALLERIA DEI CANDELABRI·DELLA GALLERIA DEGLI ARAZZI e DELLE CARTE GEOGRAFICHE·DELLE STANZE DI R

PIANTA DELLA BIBLIOTECA·DELL'APPARTAMENTO BORGIA·DEL MVSEO EGIZIO·DEL MVSEO CHIARAMONT

MVSEI·GALLERIE PoNTIFICIE
e
BIBLIOTECA APoSTOLICA VATICANA

ANNO DOM. MCMXXIV

Map of the Vatican Museums in 1924, engraving

BIBLIOGRAPHY

AA.VV., *La Pinacoteca Vaticana. Nella pittura l'espressione del messaggio divino, nella luce la radice della creazione pittorica*, Milan 1992.

AA.VV., *Raffaello nell'appartamento di Giulio II e Leone X*, Milan 1993.

F. BURANELLI – M. SANNIBALE, *Vaticano. Museo Gregoriano Etrusco*, Milan 2003.

N. DACOS, *Le Logge di Raffaello*, Rome 1986.

P.L. DE VECCHI, *La Cappella Sistina: il restauro degli affreschi di Michelangelo*, Milan 1996.

N. DEL RE (ed. by), *Mondo Vaticano. Passato e Presente*, Città del Vaticano 1995.

A. GRECO, *La Cappella di Niccolò V del Beato Angelico*, Rome 1980.

J.C. GRENIER, *Museo Gregoriano Egizio (Guide-Catalogo dei Musei Vaticani, 2)*, Rome 1993.

Guida ai Musei e alla Città del Vaticano, Città del Vaticano 2003.

P. LIVERANI, *Dal Pio-Clementino al Braccio Nuovo*, in *Pio VI Braschi e Pio VII Chiaramonti*, Acts of the International Congress (Cesena, May 1997), Bologna 1998, pp. 27-41.

P. LIVERANI, *Museo Chiaramonti (Guide-Catalogo dei Musei Vaticani, 1)*, Rome 1989.

A. NESSELRATH, *Vaticano. La cappella Sistina: il Quattrocento*, Milan 2003.

C. PIETRANGELI, *I Musei Vaticani. Cinque secoli di storia*, Rome 1985.

C. PIETRANGELI (a cura di), *Il Palazzo Apostolico Vaticano*, Florence 1992.

C. PIETRANGELI, *I dipinti del Vaticano*, Udine 1996.

D. REDIG DE CAMPOS, *I Palazzi Vaticani*, Bologna 1967.

Pianta del Secondo Piano della porzione del Palazzo Vaticano che comprende il Museo de Candelabri, Sale di Raffaello ed altri accessorj

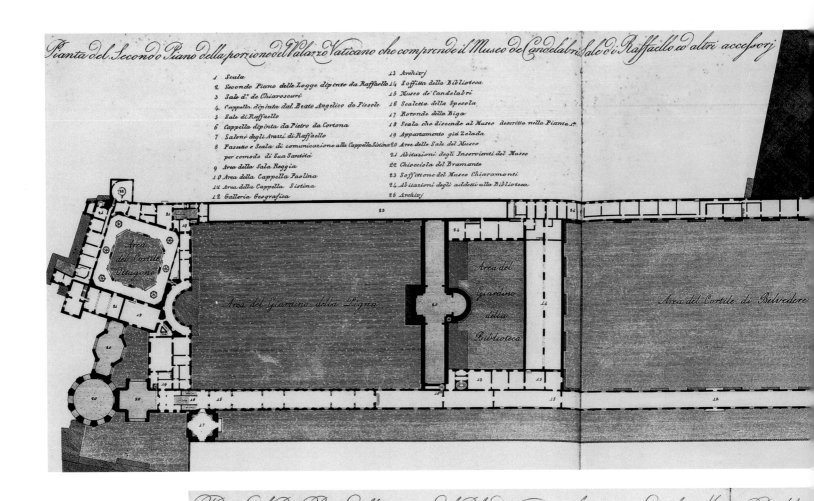

1 Scala
2 Secondo Piano delle Logge dipinte da Raffaello
3 Sale d: de Chiaroscuri
4 Cappella dipinta dal Beato Angelico da Fiesole
5 Sale di Raffaello
6 Cappella dipinta da Pietro da Cortona
7 Saloni degli Arazzi di Raffaello
8 Passetto e Scala di comunicazione alla Cappella Sistina per comodo di Sua Santità
9 Area della Sala Reggia
10 Area della Cappella Paolina
11 Area della Cappella Sistina
12 Galleria Geografica
13 Archivj
14 Soffitta della Biblioteca
15 Museo de' Candelabri
16 Scaletta della Specola
17 Rotonde della Biga
18 Scala che discende al Museo descritta nella Pianta 1ª
19 Appartamento già Zelada
20 Aree delle Sale del Museo
21 Abitazioni degli Inservienti del Museo
22 Chiocciola del Bramante
23 Soffittone del Museo Chiaramonti
24 Abitazioni degli addetti alla Biblioteca
25 Archivj

Area del Cortile Ottagono — Area del Giardino della Pigna — Area del Giardino della Biblioteca — Area del Cortile di Belvedere

Pianta del Primo Piano della porzione del Palazzo Vaticano che comprende il Museo, Bibliote...

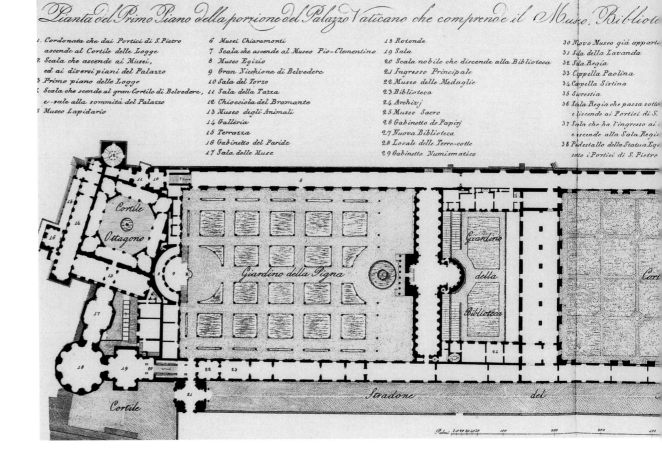

1 Cordonata che dai Portici di S. Pietro ascende al Cortile delle Logge
2 Scala che ascende ai Musei, ed ai diversi piani del Palazzo
3 Primo piano delle Logge
4 Scala che scende al gran Cortile di Belvedere e sale alla sommità del Palazzo
5 Museo Lapidario
6 Musei Chiaramonti
7 Scala che ascende al Museo Pio-Clementino
8 Museo Egizio
9 Gran Nicchione di Belvedere
10 Sala del Torzo
11 Sala della Tazza
12 Chiocciola del Bramante
13 Museo degli Animali
14 Galleria
15 Terrazza
16 Gabinetto del Paride
17 Sala delle Muse
18 Rotonde
19 Sala
20 Scala nobile che discende alla Biblioteca
21 Ingresso Principale
22 Museo delle Medaglie
23 Biblioteca
24 Archivj
25 Museo Sacro
26 Gabinetto de Papirj
27 Nuova Biblioteca
28 Locale delle Terre-cotte
29 Gabinetto Numismatico
30 Nuovo Museo già appart...
31 Sala della Lavanda
32 Sala Regia
33 Cappella Paolina
34 Cappella Sistina
35 Sacrestia
36 Sala Regia che passa sotto... e discende ai Portici di S. Pietro
37 Sala che ha l'ingresso ai... e ascende alla Sala Regia
38 Pedestallo della Statua Egizia sotto i Portici di S. Pietro

Cortile Ottagono — Giardino della Pigna — Giardino della Biblioteca — Cortile — Stradone del — Cort...

Palmi

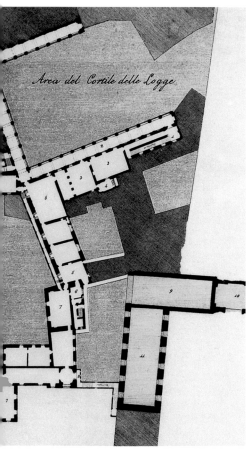

INDEX

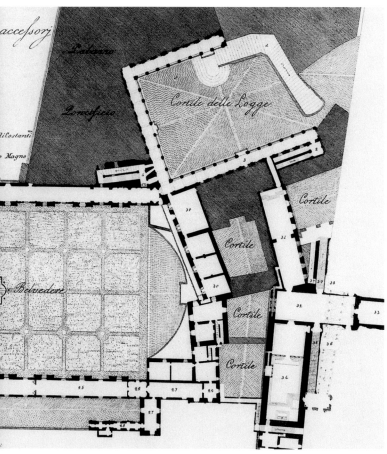

Domenico Rinaldi, Map of the Vatican Museums in 1924, engraving

*The Spiral Staircase planned by architect Giuseppe Momo and decorated with bronze balustrade made by sculptor Antonio Maraini
was inaugurated in 1932 and is today used as exit stairs*

© **Copyright 2007**
Ufficio Vendita Pubblicazioni e Riproduzioni dei Musei Vaticani, Città del Vaticano

First edition: 2007
ISBN 978-88-8271-610-3

Direzione editoriale *Francesco Riccardi, Amministratore dei Musei Vaticani*
Coordinamento editoriale *Carla Cecilia, Alessandra Murri*
Foto *Archivio Fotografico dei Musei Vaticani – Rosanna Di Pinto*

Testo *Andrea Pomella*
L'autore ringrazia Arianna Roccoli e Giuseppe Sgarzini per la preziosa collaborazione.

Il volume è stato curato da ATS Italia Editrice srl
redazione *Paola Ciogli*
ricerca iconografica *Angela Giommi*
progetto grafico, impaginazione e copertina *Sabrina Moroni*
scansioni e correzioni cromatiche *Leandro Ricci*
coordinatore tecnico *Flavio Zanda*

Questo volume è disponibile anche in italiano
Ce volume est disponible aussi en français
Dieser Band ist auch in deutscher Sprache erhäldich
Esta obra también está publicada en español

Print *Tipografia Vaticana 2007*